PRAISE FOR *THE ACTOR'S LIFE*

"I loved reading Jenna's honest and sincere appraisal of the actualities of breaking into, finding one's way, and then thriving in this business. I hope it is given out as a guidebook of sorts to any young actor when they land at LAX."
—**JON HAMM**

"How lucky for those who dream that Jenna Fischer has written this book and candidly explained the hard work, persistence, and delusion required to become a working actor. This book is generous, practical, and in the right hands will be a talisman for the deserving few who refuse to give up."
—**MATTHEW WEINER, CREATOR OF *MAD MEN***

"In *The Actor's Life*, Jenna Fischer lays out exactly what aspiring actors can expect from this crazy, unpredictable industry both practically and emotionally. Nothing is sugar-coated, nor is it cynical. It's just reality, plain and simple. At every level of success, we are all just artists trying to figure it out day by day. That's the truth."
—**CHRISTINA APPLEGATE**

"If I had Jenna's book when I was a struggling actor it would have eased the pain and encouraged my journey. This is an insightful, funny, sweet story from one actor to another; we all need a leg up, a hand to hold, and the encouragement to keep going when we truly find our passion. Jenna manages to do that and more in this very helpful guide for an actor finding their way into the business."
—**JULIANNA MARGULIES**

"Jenna Fischer's story is an excellent resource for anyone who is involved in the life of an actor. Much of this information was new to me; I have always respected the actor's journey, but now I am in awe of it. It's also entertaining from beginning to end."
—**ALLISON JONES, CASTING DIRECTOR**

THE ACTOR'S LIFE
A SURVIVAL GUIDE

JENNA FISCHER

*For Levon & Lilit—
all the best,*

BenBella Books, Inc.
Dallas, TX

Copyright © 2017 by Andycat Productions, Inc.

All rights reserved. No part of this book may be used or reproduced in any manner whatsoever without written permission except in the case of brief quotations embodied in critical articles or reviews.

BenBella Books, Inc.
10440 N. Central Expressway
Suite 800
Dallas, TX 75231
www.benbellabooks.com
Send feedback to feedback@benbellabooks.com

Printed in the United States of America
10 9 8 7 6 5 4 3 2 1

Library of Congress Cataloging-in-Publication Data is available upon request.
ISBN 978-1-944648-22-0

Editing by Debbie Harmsen and Glenn Yeffeth
Copyediting by Elizabeth Degenhard
Production editing by Monica Lowry
Proofreading by James Fraleigh, Kimberly Broderick, and Rachel Phares
Text design and composition by Aaron Edmiston
Cover design by Sarah Avinger
Cover photo by Paul Smith Photography
Makeup (cover photo) by Angela Peralta Beauty
Printed by Lake Book Manufacturing

Distributed by Two Rivers Distribution
www.tworiversdistribution.com
To place orders through Two Rivers Distribution:
Tel: (800) 343-4499
Fax: (800) 351-5073
Email: ips@ingramcontent.com

Special discounts for bulk sales (minimum of 25 copies) are available.
Please contact Aida Herrera at aida@benbellabooks.com.

For Lee, Weston, and Harper

CONTENTS

Foreword by Steve Carell ix

Introduction xiii

CHAPTER ONE
    Getting Started... 1

CHAPTER TWO
    Headshots, Getting in the Union,
    and Building Your Résumé................................. 36

CHAPTER THREE
    How to Find, Get, and Keep an Agent or Manager 79

CHAPTER FOUR
    Auditioning, Rejection, and How to Persevere.............. 102

CHAPTER FIVE
    You Got a Job! How Things Work on a
    Television or Film Set................................... 133

CHAPTER SIX
    The Journey 179

ACTOR INTERVIEWS
    Sharing the Brushstrokes 204
    Natalie Zea 206
    Sean Gunn 218
    Derek Waters 228
    Reed Birney 238
    Advice from Peers 250

    Photo Credits 252

    Acknowledgments 253

    About the Author 255

FOREWORD
BY STEVE CARELL

When I was a kid, I wanted to be either a zookeeper or a fireman. Later on, as I matured, I decided that I would operate a crane. As my crane dreams faded they were supplanted by my bulldozer phase, followed closely by my backhoe period, and finally, my dump truck passion. By then I was six years old and I knew that I had to stop playing around and commit to something practical.

Acting.

Granted, there was a brief period between ages fifteen and twenty-two when I thought I'd become a lawyer, but that madness faded quickly and I decided to pursue the noble art of Thespeaniserism (sp?). But how? What's my first move? What sort of things should I know? How do I prepare myself? Is there any source of practical information on how to approach a career in acting?

Does the woman who played Pam on *The Office* have any honest and thoughtful advice?

Yes. Yes she does.

I first met Jenna Fischer in 2004. We had both been cast in the pilot of the US remake of *The Office*, a critically acclaimed BBC show. Jenna was quiet and sweet, and within moments of our first meeting I knew that she was also a terrific actor—completely present, detailed, and subtle. She was effortlessly funny and she possessed something that I always admire in actors: she never seemed to be trying too hard. Week after week she would find complexities to her character, Pam. It never became routine or stale. I also admired the way in which Jenna could play wonderful non-verbal moments. There's a scene in season three when my character, Michael, shows up at Pam's art show. Jenna played it with such a delicate touch. She conveyed sadness, pain, joy, appreciation, and love. Silently. In about 45 seconds. She's an extremely deft, intuitive actor. I spent seven years with Jenna on the show, and the quality of her work never wavered. I also admired her professionalism. She always knew her lines, was always on time, was a great ensemble player, and her hygiene was impeccable. (I'm looking at you, Rainn Wilson.)

This book is an excellent reflection of Jenna's talent, her work habits, and her dedication to acting. Reading this book was in many ways like retracing my own career path. (Although unlike Jenna, I did briefly dabble in the sex industry.) She relates lots of good advice—from choosing headshots, to finding an agent, to preparing for an audition. Nuts and bolts stuff that every actor has to learn at some point. She also examines the psychological and emotional toll that the journey can take. Facing rejection, accepting failure, and keeping a positive mental attitude are covered in a very frank, honest way.

I completely related to Jenna's personal journey. Crappy apartments, inventive low-cost food options (mine was rigatoni with Prego), and the ever-present skepticism of friends and family. I still remember the bemused and slightly pitying looks I received at my 25th high school reunion; I told my old classmates that I'd just co-written and starred in a movie called *The 40-Year-Old Virgin*.

There is a certain resolve that a person must have to persist at something that seems intangible at times. Jenna's book gives a road map for navigating the road that every actor has to take. I wish that I had this book when I was starting out. Perhaps I would have made something out of myself.

In all honesty, it would have made life a lot easier.

INTRODUCTION

I grew up in St. Louis, Missouri. When you grow up in a place like St. Louis, saying you want to be a professional actor is the equivalent of saying you want to be a professional surfer. Not very realistic. But, apparently, no one ever told me, because as early as I can remember, I had big dreams of being an actor. In grade school I got my start when I played Toto in *The Wizard of Oz*. In case you're not familiar with the story, Toto is the dog that belongs to the lead character, Dorothy. It was a role that nobody else wanted. I guess the other kids couldn't find the value in playing the dog. But I didn't care; I liked dogs! Sure, I didn't have lines, but I had lots of stage time. See, Toto was onstage every time Dorothy was onstage, and Dorothy was the *lead*, so I was always right next to the lead! I did funny little dances with the Munchkins and barked at the Wicked Witch. Who needs lines when you can ham it up as the spunky sidekick? Then in high school I played the Fiddler in the musical *Fiddler on the Roof*. This was another role that no one else really wanted. But hey, my character opened and closed the play up on that roof. And, without the Fiddler, it would just be called *The Roof*!

At some point in my formative years, it dawned on me that an acting career wouldn't happen in St. Louis. There were only a

Fiddler on the Roof, *1991*

handful of movies filmed there during my entire childhood, among them *American Flyers*; *Planes, Trains and Automobiles*; and, for you trivia buffs, *Escape from New York*. But the idea of moving from St. Louis to Los Angeles (La La Land) or New York (The City of Broken Dreams) was daunting and scary. Hollywood in particular seemed like a million miles away, almost like another country with its own customs and currency. And if I was able to somehow get to Tinseltown, how would I even begin to break into show business? I didn't know anyone. No fancy connections. No idea how the business worked. I'd heard stories of girls being discovered at the mall. *Did that mean I should go shopping more often?* I'd heard that most movie stars had that special "it" quality. *Did I have "it"? Not likely, since my proudest acting moment was playing a dog.* I'd heard about a stand-up comedian being offered a starring role on a hit TV show. *So, that's the secret? Should I start doing standup?* (Actually, I tried standup once. The lesson I learned was to sit back down.) Nonetheless, after college I collected my theater degree, packed up my Mazda 323 hatchback, and, along with my cat, Andy, started on the long journey from St. Louis to Los Angeles.

I arrived in LA on a typical California day. The sun was shining, the sky was blue, the palm trees were swaying in the breeze. I pulled off the 101 Freeway and drove into Hollywood. It was my first day in Los Angeles and everything felt perfect. Then, nothing happened for six years. Well, some stuff happened, a lot of which you'll read about in this book. But six years is how long it took before I was finally earning a living as an actor. Six very long years. Six years of crying and accumulating debt and living in crappy apartments. Six years of small successes followed by heaps of rejection. And it would be two additional years before I landed the role of Pam Beesly on *The Office*. Eight years, then. Eight grueling years before I'd get my first big break.

During all that time in the trenches, I wish I'd had a mentor to give me advice. Someone who could put the whole daunting experience in context, who'd been through the heartache, the tears, the rejection, and made it through to the other side. Because while being an aspiring actor can be very difficult, it can also be very inspiring. There's a unique and personal awareness that comes when you're forced to dig deep, look honestly at yourself, and question your artistic resolve. And now that I've been through it, I've realized that the struggle is a natural part of the process, the profession's unique way of testing your desire and creativity. But amid all the confusion and rejection, it would have been helpful for me to have someone to pump me up, put things in context, and pass along relatable stories. So, if you're an aspiring actor (and I'm guessing you are since you're reading this book), I'd like to be that person for you.

I had an acting teacher who used to say, "If you can think of *anything* you're passionate about besides acting, do that. Your life will be better for it." And while it may sound harsh, I actually think that's very good advice. I didn't follow it because I couldn't think of anything else to do. If you're like me and can't think of anything else either, then this book is for you. And as your newly minted mentor, I'm here to tell you that you've made a noble choice, because acting is a worthwhile pursuit. I can't tell you how to make it. I can't tell you if you will be successful. But I can encourage you and, hopefully, make the journey slightly more enjoyable.

So, let's get to it. Good luck. I have faith in you.

—JENNA

CHAPTER ONE
GETTING STARTED

"The miracle isn't that I finished. The miracle
is that I had the courage to start."
—JOHN BINGHAM

I'm in Buckinghamshire, England, lying in a meadow, surrounded by fire and wreckage. My plane has just gone down in a spectacular crash landing. Bits and pieces of the plane are scattered all around me. The passengers of the plane all seem to be alive. It's 95 degrees outside and I'm wearing an orange polyester prison jumpsuit, covered in dirt and blood. Black smoke is everywhere. I'm lying here, looking at the sky. A herd of sheep saunters by.

Okay, this isn't real. I'm an actor and this is the scene of the day. The fires are real. The sheep are real. The dirt and blood are not. When I first walked onto the set I couldn't believe my eyes. The wreckage from a full-sized jetliner was strewn across a field, fires burning all

Me and actor Prasanna Puwanarajah on the set of You, Me and the Apocalypse

around. According to the script, my job was to get into a broken seat and pretend I've just crashed-landed. So I did. And as I reclined back in the seat, I couldn't help but think about what a crazy, surreal life I'm living.

It's hard to believe that I'm a working actor. Not only was I fortunate enough to spend nearly ten years shooting an iconic American television show, but now I'm living in London with my family and working with stunts and fires and car chases—and this big airplane crash. I feel like an action star. I'm so lucky. And so grateful. I have to pinch myself.

I did not grow up in a showbiz family. My parents weren't actors or musicians or writers. My father was a plastics engineer and my mother was a school teacher. Both are now retired, but they both loved what they did. My mom says she always felt a calling to be a teacher. And it showed. And if you've ever seen my dad pack a suitcase, you can immediately tell that he was meant to be an engineer.

Getting Started 3

Both of my parents were able to build careers doing what they love, and I feel like their example rubbed off on me. From a very young age, I inherently knew I had to follow my bliss.

While I knew I wanted to be an actor from the time I was a child, I was not a "child actor." I went to dance class, joined the theater club, and put on little shows in my garage, but I never acted professionally. The bulk of my childhood acting experience came as a result of auditioning for school plays. These auditions mostly ended in failure; I never got the lead roles. In fact, I barely got the supporting roles. I usually found myself being offered the obligatory consolation prize: a role in the dancing chorus. Don't believe me? Look.

Freshman year

Sophomore year

4   **The Actor's Life**

Junior year

Senior year (Fiddling my heart out. Seriously, could I be farther in the background? I don't think so.)

Needless to say, I didn't grow up with a gaggle of people convinced I was the next big acting sensation. Of course, in hindsight, my old theater teachers are happy to discuss my "obvious" talent from a young age. I'm still close to many of them and I find it hilarious when they tell me how they "saw something in me." *Yes, you saw me in the dance chorus!*

But somehow being stuck in the chorus didn't damage my resolve to give it a try professionally. In fact, it probably emboldened me. I knew I had to give it a try. No matter how difficult it seemed, I was determined to make it as an actor.

But *why* did I feel this need to try? *Why* did I want to be an actor? At the time, I never gave it a second thought. But this is an important personal question, one that I think every actor should ask themselves. And by the time you've finished this book, I believe you'll know my answer. But what about you? This profession is very demanding, both as an art form and a business, and will most likely require years of dedicated struggle. So, as you make your way through this book, I challenge you to ask yourself the same question: Why do you want to be an actor?

I can tell you off the bat, if you're chasing fame and money, you're likely to be disappointed. Even if you aren't, even if you are doing it for the love of the craft, you are likely to experience discouragement. The journey to becoming a working actor (meaning simply, an actor who makes a living through acting) is a long and difficult one that requires a lot of hard work and perseverance. But it also requires something more obscure and out of your control: luck. Without a little luck on your side, you can be the most talented actor in the world and not achieve success. That's the hard truth about this profession.

I have a friend who's been acting for more than twenty years. He's a very talented, classically trained actor, always very memorable and funny in whatever role he plays. He's not famous, although he does get recognized from time to time. But after literally hundreds of amazing performances, he still doesn't make his living from being an actor. He's still a full-time waiter.

Another friend has been earning his living as an actor since he was nineteen years old. He's now in his forties and unknown to the general public. He does theater (on and off Broadway), movies, and television shows, living basically paycheck to paycheck. Sometimes he has a good year—like the time he landed a season-long role on an award-winning television show. Sometimes he has a bad year—like the time he did a low-paying independent film with an acclaimed director that ended up never selling at the festivals. He's not rich. He's not famous. But he works and earns his living exclusively from acting. He loves it.

> "All of us have bad luck and good luck. The man who persists through the bad luck—who keeps right on going—is the man who is there when the good luck comes—and is ready to receive it."
> —Robert Collier

With most careers, the path to success is laid out for you. There is a clear set of advancements and promotions to strive for. If you're great at the job, you get rewarded. If you show up, and work above and beyond everyone's expectations, you are pretty much guaranteed to move up the ladder. Not so with acting. There is no justice in our business, no pecking order for advancement. So, then, why does it work for some and not others? A heavy dose of luck.

When I landed my role on *The Office* I had been a poor, struggling, unknown actor for eight years. I worked hard, sure, making ends meet from job to job. But other actresses were out there working just as hard as me. I had talent, they had talent. But, then, suddenly, I had luck. When Pam came along, my particular set of attributes and talents aligned perfectly for the character. I was the right person at the right time for the right job. But that's not the extent of my serendipity. If you think about it, if Ricky Gervais had never met Stephen Merchant and created the original British version of *The Office*, or if some executive in the States hadn't decided to make the American version, or if the casting director hadn't thought to bring me in for an audition, or if NBC hadn't decided to pick up the show after we made the pilot, I would probably still be out there pounding the pavement, looking for my next three lines on *Law & Order*. The fact is, I got very, very lucky.

Before I moved to Los Angeles, I thought the life of an actor seemed easy. And now, years later, I am telling you it's not. It can be rewarding, inspiring, magical, intense, terrifying, consuming, passionate, and unique. But it is not, and will not, be easy. However, just because something is difficult, doesn't mean you shouldn't do it. If you love acting, if you have a gift for acting, you should go for it. If you feel you have a talent to share with the world that is meaningful and important, you must give it a try. I believe there are steps you can take to gain an edge on the competition, and there are ways to increase your chances of being lucky. I will discuss many of these throughout the book, but in this chapter let's look at the very beginning steps of your actor's life.

> "The price of inaction is far greater than the cost of a mistake."
> —Meg Whitman

TRAINING

I believe the most important thing an aspiring actor needs is training. I graduated with a BA in theater from a tiny liberal arts college called Truman State University in Kirksville, Missouri. Kirksville is a college town. It's small and safe; you can walk everywhere. It's far enough from my hometown of St. Louis that I felt separated from my parents, but close enough that I could drive home on the weekends if I wanted. I got a great education, and I didn't leave school with a giant debt.

Theater school was *awesome*. In one class, we sat in a circle and gave one another shoulder rubs. I'm not kidding. Massage trains were part of the curriculum. Best-kept secret about becoming a trained actor! I also did exercises like stand in front of the class and roar like a lion, or move through space like a squirrel. I did a scene where I repeated the same line over and over with different intentions. These exercises might sound silly or pointless when you read them here, but trust me—they turn you into an actor. We worked on voice, movement, breaking down a character. We read tons and tons of plays and did tons and tons of scenes. Memorizing lines became second nature.

Theater school provides you the opportunity to be cast against type. When I was a senior in college I got cast as the middle sister, Meg, in *Crimes of the Heart*. She's the boozy, slutty, chain-smoking "bad girl" sister. I would never get cast as Meg in the real world. I would either be cast as Lenny, the Type-A older sister, or Babe, the wide-eyed innocent baby of the family. But a good teacher knows that the purpose of theater school is to push you out of your comfort zone. So, I was cast against type and played the wild girl. It was awesome! I went totally Method and smoked cigarettes the whole semester, wore Daisy Duke cutoffs, and went a little crazy. I loved doing that play. Did I look ridiculous? Maybe? Did anyone believe me as this character? Who cares! Look at how much fun I'm having:

Crimes of the Heart, *Truman State University 1995*

My school didn't have a film and television department. So in order to make films, a bunch of us from the theater department rented video cameras. We wrote, shot, and edited our own projects. Our biggest hit

> "Athletes, doctors, teachers—they all have to continue training to be at the top of their game. And I think the same is certainly true for actors, singers, dancers, and anyone pursuing a career as an actor."
> —Rachel Hoffman, casting director

was a satire of *NYPD Blue* that we called *KPD Blues*. It was a comedic spin on the then-popular TV cop drama, but it was also a send-up of the local Kirksville Police Department. The episodes ran on the closed-circuit college TV station that broadcast to the student center and the dorms. The station was normally reserved for the broadcast of debates and school sporting events, but we were renegades! We were the first class to create original programming. The experience of creating my own work was probably the most valuable thing I learned in school, aside from acting technique. Being able to generate work for yourself is an essential part of the process of becoming a working actor.

By the way, a number of successful actors met and collaborated in college. Christopher Reeve and Robin Williams were roommates at Juilliard. Holly Hunter and Frances McDormand were roommates at the Yale School of Drama. Wes Anderson and Owen Wilson met in a writing class at the University of Texas at Austin. From that class, they went on to make *Bottle Rocket* together, and the rest is history.

You don't have to go to theater school to become an actor, but I believe that training is essential. You may have natural talent, which is great, but having natural ability doesn't mean you don't also need to learn acting technique. Acting is a serious craft, a learned skill that needs to be developed. If you just want to be famous, become a reality star. If you want to be an actor, study acting. So, as we proceed in this book, I'm going to assume you have, or will be, taking acting classes or attending an acting conservatory. If you have, great. If you haven't, stick a bookmark in this page and get yourself in a class. In

Steve Martin's comedy course for MasterClass, he says, "I was talking to some students and they were saying some things like, 'How do I get an agent? Where do I get my headshots?' and I just thought, 'Isn't the first thing you're thinking about 'How do I be good?'" Before you embark on the business end of becoming an actor—that world of headshots and agents—you need to get good.

Picking the right class is important. All too often I hear about new actors having horrible experiences with acting classes. It is my personal opinion that acting class is *not* therapy. You don't have to share your childhood traumas in acting class, and you should not be yelled at or demeaned by an egomaniacal teacher. There is a popular acting class in Los Angeles that recruits a lot of new actors in town with big promises of stardom. It's ridiculously expensive, the class size is huge, and you spend months waiting to perform. The rumor is that you can't "graduate" until you've done at least one of the following things in class: cry, get naked, or kiss someone of the same sex. If you find yourself in a class like this, get out. Life is too short. You don't have to be abused to become a good actor—I promise! A good acting class is about stretching, learning, and discovering in a *safe, nurturing environment*. There should be no shaming, no forcing you into things that make you uncomfortable. It should provide you with lots of performance time and constructive feedback. Don't let a bad experience deter you from finding the right place to study. Good training is key to succeeding in this business. You will be competing against thousands of other actors who are also right for the role, some of whom have studied or trained with dedication. You want to be one of the ones who know what they are doing. Training is not just something you do when you are first starting out, either. It should be an ongoing commitment. Professional athletes train in the off-season. So should you.

THE BIG MOVE

Unless you already live in LA or New York, you are going to have to move if you want to be a professional actor. If your goal is to be a film or television actor, move to Los Angeles. If you want to do theater, move to New York.

But before we talk about the coasts, let's talk about the great city of Chicago. When I was starting out, a lot of people wondered if it would be easier to start off in Chicago. Chicago is a great theater town, and there are often film and television shoots there. It is home to some of the best comedy schools: iO, The Second City, and The Annoyance Theatre. It is definitely possible to be a working actor in Chicago. If you are serious about a career in comedy, Chicago is a great place to study and find your voice. When I was starting out, a common strategy was to move to Chicago, get some credits under your belt, and then take those credits to Los Angeles or New York. If you live in the Midwest and Chicago is an easy move for you, this may not be such a bad idea. I know a lot of actors who went to college in Chicago and were able to audition for commercials on the side. They were fortunate enough to earn their Screen Actors Guild–American Federation of Television and Radio Artists (SAG-AFTRA) union card this way. Or maybe you will get a great theater role and get your Actors' Equity card. You will definitely have an advantage if you are already in the union and have a few professional credits under your belt when you move to New York or Los Angeles. But let me be clear: *There is nothing easier about Chicago.* It's just as competitive as LA or New York. It may even be more competitive, because there are fewer jobs and more good actors. And the winter is brutal. If you don't believe me, take a trip there in the middle of February. Being a struggling actor is hard no matter what city you are in.

Today, a lot of people wonder if they should move to Atlanta, New Orleans, or Albuquerque. A lot of projects are shooting in these cities, which means a lot of small acting roles. A few years ago, the booming city was Detroit. Before that, Vancouver. Every few years a different city passes new tax incentives and a bunch of movies and TV shows start filming there. But then the incentives change and everyone moves on. If you already live close to one of these cities and you can use this to your advantage, I say go for it. Maybe pick a college that is close to one of these cities and try to get some professional gigs while you are in school. But no matter where you begin, eventually most actors are faced with the question of whether to move west to Los Angeles or east to New York. Because, simply put, *Los Angeles and New York are the cities with the most opportunities for the working actor*. Plus, most of the major roles—even the ones shooting in Atlanta and New Orleans—are cast out of New York and Los Angeles.

> "You just hope that you will get the opportunity to do what you love and pay your bills, and that is being a success as an actor."
> —Debra Messing

It isn't easy to pack up all your crap and move to a big city where you don't know anyone. But it must be done, because sustaining work as an actor starts with the relationships you build with local casting directors and producers. And to do that, you've got to be in their city. I wanted to be the next Diane Chambers from *Cheers*, which is why I decided to forego Chicago and move to Los Angeles. Also, if I'm being honest with myself, I wasn't sure I'd have the courage to move twice.

When I moved to LA, I rented a dingy apartment in West Hollywood. This place was beyond depressing. It was interior, which meant it was surrounded by other buildings. There was leaded glass on the windows. While great for privacy, leaded glass meant very little sunlight got through. So, it was dark. The windows cranked open with a rusty mechanism that sometimes worked and sometimes didn't. In short, it was a cave in the middle of the city. I lived there with a male friend from college and my cat, Andy, who found this living situation so depressing that he licked out patches of his fur.

Getting Started 13

My first apartment in Los Angeles (I'm not a contractor but something tells me the electrical cord running between the stove and fridge is not up to code.)

The upside of this hovel? Big and cheap. And because it was situated on the bottom floor underneath a staircase, it stayed cool. Being cool was vital to our survival because the place had no air conditioning. As for the bathroom, my visiting sister refused to shower in it because she said it looked "too scary." She still calls it "the place with the scary bathroom."

My bedroom had stained carpet, a futon mattress on the floor, and cardboard boxes as nightstands. And that's about it. After a year, my roommate built me a wooden riser for my futon mattress, using some free lumber from his theater company. It got the mattress off the floor and provided me with additional storage. If I put a comforter over the edges, it almost seemed like a real bed.

Our living room had a torn bedsheet for a window covering. Classy, right? The window was next to a busy stairwell that was constantly being used by our upstairs neighbors to get to and from their apartments. A painter lived upstairs. He never left his apartment except to take his trash to the dumpster (which was outside our front door). He eventually committed suicide. Probably due to lack of sunlight, among other things. Next door there lived an obese woman who couldn't get out of bed. She had an in-home nurse—or a series of in-home nurses—and every now and then her son would visit, and they would scream at each other in Russian.

Did I mention this was considered a pretty good apartment? It was a central location in West Hollywood, near Santa Monica Blvd. and Fairfax Blvd. There was a Laundromat around the corner, so convenient that we could walk home between the wash and dry cycles. The neighborhood was basically filled with old Russians, and it was right next to Boys Town (aka the gay section of town). Gay men and old Russians meant a young woman could walk safely by herself to and from the quick store, even at night.

If you made me live there today, I would probably pull my hair out, like my cat did. But at the time, I made the best of it. Because I was young, I was in Hollywood, and I was living my dream. (If you are thinking of moving to Los Angeles, some good spots for young actors to live are West Hollywood, Los Feliz, Silverlake, Eagle Rock, and Studio City.)

Living in the hovel was a sacrifice, but that's what it takes when you're a struggling actor. Assume there will be no luxuries. Be prepared to get your furniture from one of three places: thrift stores, garage sales, or the side of the road. Unless you have some kind of trust fund, you will not be shopping at Pottery Barn. You will be poor. (Me.) You will probably run up your credit cards and they will go into default. (Me.) If you work as a waiter, you will sometimes eat food that looks untouched off cleared plates. (Me, again.) In fact, you will eat all kinds of weird things. I have a friend who ate salt sandwiches for dinner: two pieces of bread with salt in the middle. I'm not making that up. Peanut butter was a luxury and, like I said, there were no luxuries. So, if you decide to become an actor, get ready to eat like a college student until, at least, your late twenties.

Here's a recipe to get you started:

Actor's Pizza
1 slice of bread
2 ketchup packets
1 slice of American cheese

Spread ketchup on slice of bread. Put cheese on top. Heat in microwave for 45 seconds. (If you have a toaster oven, even better.) Enjoy!

After reading about my experience in Los Angeles, you might be thinking, "Screw that! Los Angeles sounds horrible! I'm moving to New York." I love New York; it's the greatest city in the world. But just be aware that if you move there, your apartment will be smaller. I've known friends who could cook and pee at the same time because their toilet was so close to the stove. I recently saw a listing for a

New York studio apartment that had a shower *in* the kitchen. Not next to the kitchen, but *in* the kitchen. It was being listed for $1,795 a month. "Will this small closet-like apartment save me money?" you ask. Nope. It will be *more* expensive than the dingy Los Angeles cave. It could possibly be in a building with seven flights of stairs and no elevator. And you will probably share it with three other roommates. The good news: You don't need a car in New York, which means you also don't need car insurance. Right there, two LA essentials that you won't need to budget for. Plus, all of the city walking can serve as your exercise plan—no gym membership needed! It's true, some subway stairwells smell like urinals, but that's okay—you can't afford to ride the subway anyway!

So, if your motivation for becoming an actor is because you are hoping to be rich, change careers now. Most actors barely earn a living wage from their acting work. According to the Screen Actors Guild, the median income for a working actor is $52,000 a year. But **most of the SAG-AFTRA membership earns less than $7,000 a year from acting.** Only 5 percent (of actors in SAG-AFTRA) earn more than $100,000. These are just the statistics for union actors. It's safe to assume non-union actors are earning even less.

But let's just pretend you earn $52,000 a year from acting. You will not bring home $52,000 a year.

$52,000 Annual Gross Income
- $5,200 agent commission
- $5,200 manager commission
- $12,600 average taxes

$29,000 take-home pay per year = No couches from Pottery Barn

The Nest Egg

If you can move to Los Angeles or New York with a nest egg, I highly recommend it. These cities are expensive. Not only will you need money for rent, groceries, phone, cable, and so on, but you'll also need money to grow your new acting business. You'll need money for headshots, more acting classes, membership fees to websites, and maybe even to help fund your own independent project. You'll need money to help you get through the poor-yet-working actor phase of your career. This phase can last a long time, so build that nest egg!

My Diary, 1998

Please enjoy this sampling of my very real, very sobering, journal entries from my early years in LA.

June 15, 1998 (2 Years in LA)
I just started a full-time job and I am freaking out!! Here I am—in LA—it's been 2 years and I'm feeling lazy about my career. Fuck! I am so goddamn nervous right now. I'm nervous just writing in this journal. No one will ever see it, yet I'm nervous. That's probably my problem right there—I'm nervous even around myself! I judge myself too much. So I have this job to get my money situation under control and I have a pretty good agent. But I should really be out hustling for myself, I think. I am going to try and write. I am giving myself an assignment to write one journal page every morning for one week! Well, back to work. I feel a little better. This journal is a good idea already. Plan, Decide, Act. There it is!

June 16, 1998 (The next day)

Okay, so I didn't get up and write this morning. But I did walk after work, arrange dinner, grocery shop and paint my toenails. I *really* really wanted a callback for this Disney cruise thing. One month traveling on a cruise ship!! Does it get any better than that?! Callbacks are tomorrow so I'm assuming I didn't get it. So, of course, I'm reviewing everything I did to figure out why I sucked.

July 15, 1998

I get paid today. Now I get to figure out where this paycheck goes. I owe my dad $110. I owe the DMV $366. And I owe Mastercard $80. Now, I have a few choices—One, I pay off DMV completely and have a registered car. Or, I pay the minimum balance due on my MC which is about $325 or so. I need to refinance this card.

100	In bank
650	Get Paid
750	
-360	Mastercard/Car
-110	Dad
-51	Parking Ticket (forgot about that)

$229 to live on for two weeks. I can do that. It means grocery shopping, not eating out, and very little spending. While hopeful, this is also making me anxious. New subject—I'm thinking of painting my room orange. Great, now I'm thinking about how I can't afford to. Never mind that.

After college and before moving to Los Angeles, I spent a year living in St. Louis with my parents. This was the longest year of my life. The. Longest. Year. It was pretty awful going from my free-spirited college lifestyle to living in my parent's house again. Honestly, I don't think they were too thrilled either. I would get home after midnight, and the next morning we'd all pretend like I hadn't been out having sex with my boyfriend.

But I'm grateful to them; they were generous enough to let me live at home and save all my earnings for my voyage to Los Angeles. I spent that year working as a secretary/receptionist in a small business that specialized in selling marine audio equipment. I made coffee, answered the phones, helped the salesmen with their PowerPoint presentations, did the filing, processed invoices, and handled customer returns. Essentially, I was Pam. The cool thing about the life of an actor is that many pointless and mundane experiences actually become important moments that you'll reference later in your career. The year I spent working at the marine audio business totally prepared me for the role of Pam. Of course, I didn't know this at the time, I was just slogging it out with bad coffee and itchy pantyhose. But it's interesting how the struggles can pay off in the long run. You may not know how, but in a magical twist of fate, what you're dreading doing today could inspire a role years from now.

> "You can have it all. Just not all at once."
> —Oprah Winfrey

I graduated from college in August 1995. To avoid being stuck at home forever, I gave myself a goal. I would either move to Los Angeles in May 1996, or when I had saved $10,000. So, I spent the ensuing months working and saving. When May finally came, I had $8,000. It wasn't quite the $10,000 I had imagined, but I couldn't wait any longer. I packed my car and hit the road. I can still remember the looks on my parents' faces as I pulled out of the driveway, a mixture of fear and relief. Mostly relief that I was out of the house.

I drove to LA with my $8,000, feeling smart and prepared for my new life. I completely expected to be a rich and famous actress within two years of moving to Los Angeles. (If we are being honest, I expected it to happen within the first six months, but I pretended like I expected it to take two years so I didn't seem too arrogant.) I had it all planned out. First, I would meet with my roommate's commercial agent. I figured she'd meet with me, love me, and sign me. I'd then immediately book a national commercial, which would get me my SAG-AFTRA card, plus a nice chunk of cash. Then I'd use my ace-in-the-hole. My mom had a friend from church whose son worked at one of the top talent agencies, the William Morris Agency. He would be my movie agent. He'd take me to parties where I'd meet producers and directors, who would quickly notice my obvious star quality. I'd be easy to cast because I'd tell them I could do comedy or drama. I felt sorry for all the suckers without connections like mine. Stardom, here I come!

And here's the reality: After six months, my $8,000 was gone. I'd used it for rent, groceries, headshots, movie tickets, lunches, and a new engine for my car. I wasn't even able to afford new shoes, even though my current pair had a hole in the bottom. (I remember this because it was the year of the big El Niño storm and my left foot was always wet.) As far as my career plan, my roommate's commercial agent wouldn't even meet with me. My mom's church friend's son was a *literary* agent at the William Morris Agency, which means he represented writers, not actors. Oops. So, my plan to attend glitzy parties and wow the bigwigs was nothing but a pipe dream. Here I was, six months into my big Hollywood move, and nobody knew I existed. I felt cut-off, confused, and alone. I cried myself to sleep more than I'd want my mom to know. The thought of quitting was constantly on my mind, probably five times a day. But, the fact is, I was too embarrassed to go home. I'd basically told everyone I was going to be this big star in Hollywood, and I couldn't imagine facing them now. I was humbled and humiliated. But what could I do? I was out of ideas. I had done everything I could think of to "network" and meet people. I had asked every friend with an agent to refer me for representation, but none of the agents would meet with me. How had I hit rock bottom so quickly? What was I doing wrong?

BE A JOINER

When I first moved to Los Angeles, I had a chip on my shoulder. I didn't sign up for acting classes or join a theater company. My thinking was, "I just graduated with a theater degree. What do I need acting classes for?" So I sat on my couch reading *Backstage* magazine, submitting myself for countless auditions, and waiting for the phone to ring. Meanwhile, my roommate joined a theater company. It seemed like all he did was grunt work: building sets, cleaning the theater, taking tickets. I thought, "I didn't come here to clean up after other actors! I came here to *be* the actor!" I was so indignant. So, while I laid around the hovel, my roommate was being creative. I remember he banded together with people he'd met at his theater company, and they started writing and shooting their own stuff. He was busy all the time, constantly stepping over me as he walked out the door.

My roommate was doing it right. He was living the life of an artist. Me? I was living the life of a righteous hermit. While he spent his nights and weekends in an active, thriving, creative environment, I was home. Alone. Watching reruns of *Law & Order*. I was very isolated. Very self-involved. I was reading plays, working on accents, watching movies; one weekend I decided to rent every movie that Diane Keaton had ever done. All great stuff, but I was alone. And that made everything harder. I thought I was being "focused." I thought I was being "strategic."

Listen, I was not a snob about what I would do as an actor. I was willing to shoot student films for free. I was willing to do industrial commercials. I would do a play reading. If it involved acting, I was there. What I didn't understand was the importance of participating in a creative environment on a regular basis, in finding a group of people with whom I could share a collective artistic life. My life changed when I finally found this. And the way I found this was by joining things. I volunteered to run the box office at a theater company. I joined an improv class. I took an on-camera acting class. I met like-minded artists and we started doing our own projects on the side. Sometimes I got to act in the projects, sometimes I made the props. It didn't matter. We all wanted the same thing and kept each other busy.

> "Successful people are always looking for opportunities to help others. Unsuccessful people are always asking, 'What's in it for me?'"
> —Brian Tracy

If you want to be an actor, you must live an artistic life. You must find ways to express your artistic life with others. Artistic lives are full of risk. I wasn't risking much by spending my Saturday nights watching John Cassavetes movies and feeling intellectually superior for having done it. Listen, I'm glad I did all that. I love that I had a year where I was obsessed with silent films and another when I rented every Academy Award–winning movie from 1970 to 2000. Sometimes you need that stuff. You need to disappear to keep yourself from going totally bonkers. But I also know that when this was *all* I was doing, I was stalled. I wasn't in motion. I wasn't with other artists, growing. I was on the sidelines, watching.

On a very practical level things started moving forward for me career-wise when I started being a joiner. I volunteered for a small part in a friend's showcase and I ended up getting a manager. I joined a theater company and an agent came to our play and signed me. But that's not why I'm telling you to join things. For now, joining things is about building up the emotional network you need to make it for the long haul. It's about finding your tribe of artists who will get you through the dark times.

Most actors and artists are natural hermits. We hate talking to people. We are weirdly antisocial. But you've got to fight the urge to spend all day alone. Get off your computer and get into a class. Volunteer as a theater usher. Be a production assistant on someone's short film. Sign up for a forty-eight-hour film project or twenty-four-hour play festival. Find *anything* and join it. Even if you have a theater degree, get yourself in a class. Just because college is over doesn't mean you're done learning. In fact, you're only just beginning. Find something that interests you. Do you love comedy? Sign up for an improv class!

Find other artists like yourself who are new in town and embrace one another. You will need this. Create a family of weird, creative, supportive people. Sustaining work as an actor starts with the relationships you make with other artists. Everyone starts somewhere. Every big-name actor was an "unknown" at one point in his or her career. Building a successful career is not about getting in good with the people who are already established. It's about creating the next big thing with the people just like you. Do you know where Amy Poehler met Tina Fey? Improv class. Be a joiner.

DAY JOBS AND THE IMPORTANCE OF LYING

When you are just getting started, especially the first year, you probably won't have seven auditions a week. Thus, you probably won't be booking acting jobs. You will need to get a day job to pay your bills. My advice is to go ahead and look for that day job right away. Don't be like me. Don't sit around doing nothing, spending your nest egg. Get some income, so you can save the nest egg and only spend little bits of it when necessary. If you have money coming in, you can use your nest egg to supplement times when you must quit your day job in order to take a low-paying acting job. The less you have to stress about money, the better. Getting a day job is a pretty standard part of any acting career. It doesn't mean you've "failed."

Look at some of the jobs successful actors did to earn money in their early days:

Johnny Depp: telemarketer
Michelle Pfeiffer: supermarket cashier
George Clooney: shoe salesman
Sandra Bullock: bartender
Eva Mendes: fast food cashier
Jim Carrey: janitor
Jennifer Aniston: waitress
Hugh Jackman: party clown
Tom Cruise: hotel bell hop
Andrew Garfield: Starbucks barista
Brad Pitt: wore a chicken suit and danced in front of El Pollo Loco

Finding the right day job is an adventure all in itself. Be strategic about what kind of job you get; you will need one with flexibility. The best jobs for aspiring actors are night and weekend jobs: hotel desk clerk, hotel bellman, valet, waiter, caterer, bartender, dog walker, tutor, tape logger, babysitter—all very popular jobs for actors. Or early morning positions, like a barista at a coffee shop, so your day is free by noon. Jobs like these keep your weekdays free for meetings, auditions, classes, and acting work.

If you can't decide which day job to go for, don't worry. Chances are, you will have many, many different day jobs. Part of this is because you might book an acting job and need to quit your day job (or get fired) to take the part. Or, maybe it's because day jobs generally suck and you feel the need to shake things up. Most of the time you're just scrambling to make money any way you can, whenever you can make it. I had countless day jobs.

Getting Started

Most of my day jobs were office-related. Ironic, I know. Thanks to a mandatory typing class in high school I can type eighty-five words per minute with 90 percent accuracy. I signed up at a temp agency in downtown Los Angeles. I took short-term office assignments to pay the bills. They paid better than minimum wage. I usually covered for secretaries and receptionists on vacation. Week-long assignments at most. I had boring jobs where I answered the phone and took messages, but I also had some really cool assignments: One time I worked on the complaint line for a big-time soda company. It was my job to listen to people's complaints and then mail them coupons for free soda. Another time, I worked for a group of psychologists who performed psychological evaluations on people applying for high-ranking corporate jobs. My job was to transcribe their evaluations. It was fascinating.

Here is a picture of me at one of my many day jobs as an administrative assistant.

I supplemented my temping income by doing catering jobs on the weekends. Catering might be the best job an aspiring actor can get. Most catering jobs are evenings and weekends. The pay is decent. The work is easy. They almost always have leftover food you can eat at the end of your shift. If you attended a wedding reception at the Calamigos Equestrian Center in Burbank in 1997 there is a good chance I brought you your plate of chicken. And if you didn't like that chicken, you are crazy. Because that chicken was *goooood*. I ate it every Saturday night for an entire year and I never got tired of it.

I tried to find every way to make money and still have time to pursue my dream of acting. I even worked as a telephone psychic for about a week. I saw an ad in the back of the LA Weekly. It said, "Are you naturally intuitive? Work from home as a telephone psychic." I called the number. This was my interview:

Psychic Job Interviewer: Are you naturally intuitive?
Me: Sure. I would say I'm pretty intuitive.
Psychic Job Interviewer: Can you read tarot cards?
Me: Yeah. (Lie.)
Psychic Job Interviewer: Great. Here is your dial-in number. You can activate any time, twenty-four hours a day. Calls will be routed to your house. You work as much or as little as you want. Remember, the first five minutes of every call are free. Keep people on the phone longer than five minutes. You only get paid after the first five minutes. Got it?
Me: Yeah.

That was it. I was a telephone psychic. I went out and bought a book on astrology and one on tarot card reading. After skimming the books, I dialed in and activated my number. Calls started coming immediately. I did my best, but I wasn't very good at it. Mostly because of my MCG—Midwestern Catholic Guilt. After five minutes, I felt compelled to remind people that their free minutes were up. Most would then hang up immediately. If they did stay on the phone, I felt horrible. The calls I received fell into two camps: teenagers who were probably going to get in trouble when their parents got the phone bill, and lonely old people. The longer these people stayed on the phone the worse I felt. I did my best to be entertaining and positive. I think I often gave very good advice. But, eventually I stopped dialing in. And I never collected my paycheck. It felt like dirty money.

You should pick a day job you can quit with no consequences. I don't recommend working for a family member or friend unless you are willing to piss them off when you skip your shift, or miss a deadline at the last minute because you booked an acting gig. I also don't recommend working for a casting office or talent agent. You need a job you can sacrifice if it comes down to it. You came to be an actor, so you need to be able to cut the day job loose if needed!

A lot of times people are hesitant to hire aspiring actors because they know you'll leave them in the lurch if a big opportunity comes along. So, here is the dilemma: Do you tell your day job the truth? Do you tell them that you are, in fact, not interested in being a data entry technician/hotel clerk/waiter, but that you are actually pursuing an acting career? Well, it depends. I always chose to be honest. I lost some jobs because of it. During my countless interviews, I would always tell them I was an aspiring actor and might need flexibility to attend auditions. Most of the time the person would have to keep themselves from laughing. One time a guy said, "Yeah, you and everyone else." And I said, "No, really, I'm really doing it." And he said, "If you ever get an audition we will deal with it. But I don't think it will be a problem." Wow. Thanks for that. When I finally *did* get an audition and asked to leave work early one Tuesday, he said, "Well, what happens if you get the job? How long would you be gone?" And I said, "Two days." And he said, "If you go on the audition, don't bother coming back." And I said, "Okay." And on Tuesday at 3 PM, I left. And I didn't go back. Nor did I book the acting job.

That's when I learned how to become a very good liar, which I rationalized by saying it was a way to practice my acting skills. I still told the truth at my job interviews. I said I was an aspiring actor. But then I lied when I got auditions that interfered with my work hours. I found that jobs had no problem letting you miss a few hours for a doctor's appointment or other errands: "Sure, you can leave early to pick up your sister at the airport." But they *hated* when you needed the exact same amount of time off for an audition.

If I had an audition at 10:30 AM on Wednesday, I'd call into work at 9 AM and say "Oh, my God! I was just in a car accident! I have no car! It's being towed. My friend can bring me to work at noon. Is that okay? I'm *so sorry*!" And then I'd get to work and complain about a headache from the accident, just to make it convincing. If I booked a one-day acting job, I'd tell my boss that I needed emergency dental surgery and the only day they could see me was whatever day I was scheduled to shoot. If they pushed back, I'd cry. I'd say I couldn't sleep another night with the pain. Ha. Oh, man.

Need a quick last-minute excuse, ladies? There is nothing better than a trip to the OB/GYN. No one argues with you when you say you need to see the OB/GYN. You start by saying you have an "annual check-up," and then follow up with "procedures" and "additional testing" if you book the gig. Am I ashamed of this? No! Did I use my gender to gain an advantage? Yes. Is it unfair because men can't do it? Yes and no. First of all, talk to me about fair when women start earning more than seventy cents to every man's dollar. And, secondly, advice to the men out there: Going to see your doctor for a "prostate check" is just as wonderfully vague and cringy as a woman's trip to the OB/GYN. You can be sure you'll get out of work with no resistance.

My cat ran away, my kitchen window was smashed with a rock in the middle of the night, my car got the boot, and I think my grandfather died like four times one year. To my bosses, I had the worst luck of any person on the planet.

So, I guess this is the section of the book where Jenna Fischer admits she's a liar. It's true. My lies were an essential part of staying employed while pursuing my acting career. But it wasn't just the lies that kept me employed. I'm also a very, very good worker. I always got my work done. I did it well. I was a valuable employee, which is an important part of the day job experience. Even though it's a temporary job, do it well. Avoid the temptation to be stingy and think you're "saving your energy" for your "real" job of acting. I'm a strong believer in the idea that abundance breeds abundance. You will be better prepared to give your acting career 110 percent if you are already working at that level at your day job.

THE MOLLY SHANNON STORY

Sometimes, your day job becomes a path to something totally unexpected. Like the time my day job led me to Molly Shannon. I was working one of my countless transcription jobs. But this one was different: Instead of transcribing medical jargon or boring academic lectures, I was a transcriber for the Television Critics Association's annual press event. This event happens every fall in Los Angeles. Every major television network presents their newest lineup of television shows to the Critics Association through a series of press conferences. The producers, directors, and stars for each new television series sit on a stage and answer questions from the press about their show. The hope is that if you can dazzle the press with a great presentation, it will create good buzz about your new series. My job was to attend the press conferences, produce a written short-hand account of the panel, and then transcribe the whole thing with the help of an audio tape. We turned over the transcriptions to the press panel, which used them to write their articles. It was an *awesome* job!

I saw tons of celebrities. I got to sit and listen to industry professionals talk about their work—*and* I got paid for it! The days were long, ten to twelve hours. The transcribing part was kind of grueling. They had just one hotel room for all of the transcribers to share. They cleared the room of all furniture and replaced it with ten desks and computers. To say it was cramped was an understatement. You had to keep your elbows in while typing or you would bump your neighbor. Do you know how much heat ten desktop computers from the late 1990s produce? A lot.

We were each assigned two to three press conferences each day. We got room service for lunch and usually a big plate of cookies for dessert. But the best part of the job was that we were allowed to attend the nightly industry "parties" at the hotel, if we finished our work on time. This blew my mind.

> "In the middle of difficulty lies opportunity."
> —Albert Einstein

The "parties" were basically made up of four types of people: the celebrities/creators of television shows, the press, the network suits, and transcribers who got their work done early. There was live music, people were dressed up, drinks were in hand, hors d'oeuvres were passed—it was exactly how you'd imagine a fancy Hollywood party to be.

I've been putting "parties" in quotes because what I didn't realize at the time was that these weren't really parties. They were work. The celebrities weren't having any fun. How could they be? They were surrounded by reporters holding little tape recorders asking prying questions. The network suits were working hard to impress the television critics so they could promote their shows. And the press was tired. They sat through long days of presentations. And now they were doing their best to get some sort of exclusive quote or scoop so they had something different to offer than just the same transcription page everyone else got. Everyone was working. Except me. I was done working! I got to stand around and take it all in. I didn't care that it wasn't a real party. I was getting an insider look at the Hollywood machine at work. And I got free food!

Of all the "parties," the one I most wanted to attend was the *Saturday Night Live* party. We'd heard a rumor that the whole cast of *Saturday Night Live* would be there. I desperately wanted to see, and maybe even meet, some of my comedy idols. The *SNL* "party" was an early one; it started at 5 PM. This caused a dilemma for me because we were only allowed to crash the parties if we had finished our work for the day, and we were *never* finished by 5 PM. I had to figure out how to leave work early and sneak into the party without anyone knowing. I needed a better excuse than a lost cat or parking ticket problem. This required something more dramatic. That's when I got my big idea. I decided I would pretend I was sick and ask to go home early, then stop by the party on my way out. It was a bold plan that required a grand performance. I was up for it. After all, I was an actress, wasn't I?

The party was on Thursday evening. I began to lay the groundwork for my ruse on Wednesday morning, innocently sniffling while I transcribed in the sweltering hotel room. By Wednesday afternoon I had upped the drama and was coughing, announcing to my co-workers that I felt achy and congested. It seemed to be working, so on Thursday morning I went full "Method actor" and wore no makeup to work. In fact, I even put a little yellow cream makeup from my college Ben Nye makeup kit under my eyes to make them look sallow. (Oh my God, as I'm writing this I'm realizing how completely crazy I was back then!)

Upon seeing my appearance, my boss took me aside and said, "Hey, you don't look so good." I said, "Yeah, I've been feeling this come on for a couple of days now, but I think I'm okay. I'll stick it out." Haha! Now that the hook was set, I slowly degraded my condition as the day went on, slouching deeper in my chair and complaining of a headache. It was a shameless performance, but it worked. By 4 PM my boss was insisting that I go home and get some rest. I protested a little but then "reluctantly" agreed and gathered my things.

Feeling like Meryl Streep, I left the hotel and walked to my car, which was parked on a nearby side street. Behind the seat I had stashed supplies for my transformation: baby wipes, a makeup bag, a party dress, and heels. I washed my face with the baby wipes, did my makeup and changed clothes, all while crammed in the passenger seat of my car. Within fifteen minutes, I was party ready. As I approached the hotel security, I realized a little detail I hadn't figured out, how to get back *into* the hotel. There was security everywhere, all charged with the task of protecting the celebrities inside from weirdos attempting to sneak in and bug them (me). The only way in was through the main entrance, which was just past the crowded red carpet. Again, for security reasons, you couldn't just stroll up to this red carpet. You had to drive up, and cars needed a special access pass to get all the way through. I still had my work pass, but that only got me in the back entrance, a precarious path that could get me discovered. I was stuck.

That's when I noticed a long line of limos sitting across from the hotel. I walked up to one of the drivers and asked what he was doing. He said they were paid to drive the celebrities to the events, drop them at the red carpet, and then wait a few hours until they were done. I noticed his access pass in the window and asked him if there was *any* way he would be willing to drive me up to the red carpet and drop me off. (Again, I'm aghast at how nuts I was back then!) He smiled and said, "Sure! Hop in!" He drove me to the entrance and even opened the door for me. What a cool guy! I felt like a star.

And that is how I walked my first red carpet. Well, sort of. Here's a little-known fact: There are two lanes on every red carpet. The front lane for the celebrities, where the photographers scream their name. And the back lane is for guests and assistants. I guess I wasn't feeling *that* crazy because I walked the back lane. But nonetheless, I had red carpet under my feet. I felt so fancy! And also so empowered that the limo drop-off ploy had worked.

Once in the lobby, I headed directly to the *Saturday Night Live* party. It was pretty surreal walking into that room, suddenly surrounded by all of my favorite comedians. There I was, sipping a wine spritzer and eating off the same buffet table as Norm Macdonald. It was awesome.

As I perused the room, I noticed Molly Shannon was nearby. Jackpot. I loved this woman. She was (and still is) one of my acting idols, and I wanted so badly to meet her. She was surrounded by press, so I crossed the room and carefully inserted myself into the circle.

I stood and waited, nodding along as Molly answered questions. But after waiting a few minutes, I became so desperate to have her notice me that I started cracking jokes. Awful jokes. I vaguely remember a joke about traffic and one about boobs. It was seriously so horrible and cringy and awkward I can barely think about it without getting hives. It didn't take long before I started getting the evil eye from the reporters. So, I finally shut up and listened politely.

> "Ask for what you want and be prepared to get it."
> —Maya Angelou

Eventually the press walked away, and I seized my chance to have Molly all to myself. I said, "Hi, I'm not really supposed to be here. I'm an aspiring actress, new to LA, and I just wanted to say that I really love what you do." Now, Molly could have just been polite and said, "Thanks, nice to meet you." Or she could have blown me off. After all, I was the weirdo party crasher telling boob jokes! But she didn't. She turned to face me, looked me in the eyes, and said, "Don't give up. Whatever you do. Just don't give up, okay? It took me ten years to get on *SNL*. I walked around and no one knew who I was. Then I got on *SNL* and it all changed overnight. You just never know. So don't give up. Ten years. *Ten* years. It's hard, okay? Good luck. You can do it."

I'm not overstating things when I say that this moment was one of the most important moments of my budding career. I had been in Los Angeles for a very long year, a year that was so hard and personally challenging that I had started to doubt that I could ever make it. But here was Molly Shannon telling me it took her a decade to get noticed. She's like the funniest, most talented woman ever, and it took her *ten years*! Finally, someone who told it like it was! Someone who let me know that even when you have talent it can take a long time, that an acting career doesn't just happen overnight. It takes time. It takes work. And she told me not to give up. She was now, officially, my hero.

> "Keep away from the people who try to belittle your ambitions. Small people always do that, but the really great make you feel that you, too, can become great."
> —Mark Twain

I shook her hand and started walking away, deep in a daze of excitement and inspiration. I was so far gone that I bumped into a fellow partygoer and spilled wine spritzer all over my dress. It was a little embarrassing, clearly my fault. I turned to apologize to the partygoer and was completely shocked to see who it was: my boss. Yep. That boss! The one I had lied to. It turned out the group had decided to take a break and go to the party. All of my co-workers were there, staring at me in a party dress covered in wine spritzer. And not the least bit sick.

My boss simply said, "Feeling better?" And I said, "Yeah." Long pause. Then I said, "I'm guessing I should not come in tomorrow?" And he said, "You guessed right!" So I was fired at the *SNL* party. And, man, *was it worth it*! That advice from Molly Shannon was so inspirational, it helped me get through the subsequent years of struggle. If I needed a pick-me-up, my mom would get on the phone with me and say, "Just remember what Molly told you, honey! It took her ten years!"

Let's cut to ten years later. I'm at the movie premiere of my film *Walk Hard*, my first starring role in a major studio film, opposite John C. Reilly. My co-stars in the movie? Tim Meadows and Chris Parnell, both from *SNL*. And guess who came to the premiere to support them? Molly Shannon! At the after-party, I went over and told her the story from years ago. I thanked her, full of gratitude. We hugged. And then I pulled a photographer over to get our photo.

The trick to surviving the big move and your first year as an actor is finding the secret value of shitty situations. Because, unfortunately, there will be a lot of shitty situations. A common trait among successful working actors is their ability to keep working on their craft,

Getting Started 35

no matter what. They do this by viewing the dumpy apartment and crappy day job as an opportunity for access to people and stories outside of their normal routines. They *use* the experiences. If you have an annoying co-worker who's incessantly talking about himself, turn him into a character for your improv class. If you have a painfully long daily commute, use it to practice accents or to listen to podcasts by artists you admire. When you are able to use your experiences to feed your creativity and passion for acting, it doesn't seem as hard. Mining for gold is not easy. But if you do it long enough, you get to be the person who found gold.

CHAPTER TWO
HEADSHOTS, GETTING IN THE UNION, AND BUILDING YOUR RÉSUMÉ

"I didn't get there by wishing for it or hoping for it, but by working for it."
—ESTEE LAUDER

When I arrived in Los Angeles, my first strategy was to find a film and television agent, also known as a "theatrical agent." Between my hours of movie-watching, cereal-eating, and savings-draining, I sent out countless headshots to theatrical agents, along with letters asking for an introductory meeting. It seemed like the right thing to do. After all, agents are the portal to auditions and auditions are the portal to jobs, so . . . the least I could do was get myself an agent, right? Well, it seemed easy on paper, but the reality was a frustrating saga of disappointment.

I was talented. I was trained! Why couldn't I get these agents to meet with me? Well, first off, I had barely any experience and I wasn't in the Screen Actors Guild. Most agents will not take on non-union clients because they can't get them professional work. My only credits were from college and summer stock theater, which basically mean nothing to an agent in Hollywood. Still, I thought an agent would look at my résumé and see my potential. Isn't that the story I'd heard my whole life? The talented unknown actor is discovered by an enthusiastic agent who nurtures her and slowly turns her into a mega-star? Yeah, it's not that easy, Jenna. Not in the real world.

In the real world, agents want to make money. There's a reason it's called show *business*. Agents are very selective about their clients. And they have to be, because they only make money if the client makes money. They get 10 percent of an actor's salary. So, if you aren't in a position to make them money, they aren't interested. Such are the demands of their job. Good agents, the ones who are plugged in and successful, need an actor who is ready to work. So, let's get you ready to work.

STEP ONE: HEADSHOTS

Headshots. Every actor needs them, and every actor dreads them. So, what are headshots, anyway? They're exactly what the name implies: a photo of your head. Sounds rather cold and clinical, doesn't it? Perhaps that's why actors hate getting them. It took me several attempts before I felt like I'd really nailed it. For a long time, I didn't know the qualities that made up a good headshot. I thought it was as simple as wearing my favorite outfit and picking the prettiest picture of me. Oh, it is so much more than that.

Your headshot is the first thing an agent or casting director will see of you, so it must stand out from the sea of hundreds they look at every day. When going through headshot submissions, they flip through them very quickly, so your picture needs to pop. The next time you are in the grocery store, head on over to the cereal aisle and look at all the different cereal boxes. Many of them are virtually identical to one another in terms of ingredients, so cereal companies have to rely on other factors to grab your attention. This is why they've spent millions of dollars on *packaging*. If acting is the business, you are the product, and your headshot is the packaging. You can be the most talented actor on the planet, but if you have a crappy headshot, you may never get the chance to show off your chops.

My first and best advice for getting a good headshot is to *hire a professional headshot photographer*. Do not use your friend, your smartphone, your dad, or the portrait studio at Sears for your headshot photo. You must have a professional photographer who specializes in taking *headshots*. Model shots and portraits are something else entirely. You want professional headshots.

Your headshot needs to look like you. This advice probably seems obvious, but you would be surprised at how many actors have headshots that vaguely resemble themselves. A good headshot conveys how you look on a regular day, not your best day. It's not a Glamour Shot. It should just be you, not the prettiest or most handsome version of you, or the youngest or the sexiest. You want it to be you. Just good ol' regular you.

Casting directors expect you to look as advertised. If you have a beard when you take your headshots, be prepared to be an actor with a beard. If you cut or color your hair, you'll need new headshots to match your new look. If you are wearing glasses in your headshot, you better wear them to the audition too.

Headshots, Getting in the Union, and Building Your Résumé

Back when I was a struggling actor, I would usually go to auditions after being at work most of the day. Most likely I'd have to drive across town, which meant sitting in traffic for about an hour, in a car that had no air conditioning. Usually I'd drive with the windows down, which meant I'd sweat through my clothes while my hair was blown into a ratty, tangled mess. Once I arrived, I'd change clothes in my car and attempt to pull myself together using my rearview mirror, a portable curling iron, and Wet Wipes. My headshot had better not be glamorous.

This brings me to my best piece of advice regarding headshots, compliments of my friend, casting director Mara Casey: *Know what you are selling*. Mara was the casting director for the television show *Gilmore Girls*, among other productions. She has looked at thousands of headshots and seen both the good and the bad. When I asked her, she said her biggest headshot pet peeves occur when she receives a headshot in which the actor is a) looking away from camera, b) covered in shadows, or c) making a funny face.

Just look honestly into the lens. If that feels vulnerable, then be vulnerable. But don't try to ham it up or be artsy. Just be you. But most importantly: Know what you are selling. Mara suggests picking five adjectives that best describe the kind of characters you might *easily* play. And then ask yourself, does your headshot convey those five adjectives?

I know what you might be thinking: "I can play anything! I'm a trained actor!" But acting in the entertainment business is about typecasting and gut reactions, especially when you are starting out. If you look naturally sweet and naïve in real life, you aren't going to be cast as a drug-addicted career criminal. You just aren't. At least not at first. Trust me. I tried. You need to have a headshot that easily typecasts you.

A great way to figure out your five adjectives is to ask friends, relatives, your agent (we'll get to finding one in chapter three), or even people who don't know you very well what adjectives they would use to describe their first impression of you. Try to get a headshot that matches those adjectives.

Jenna Fischer: A History in Headshots

Okay, it's my turn to get vulnerable. And when you see my first headshots, you'll see why. I wasn't lying when I said it took me years to figure this stuff out. Ready to see some mistakes? Let's have a look.

Here's my first headshot, the one I used when I first arrived in Los Angeles:

What five things does this headshot tell you about me?

Hi, I'm new in town.
I have curly hair.
I'm not a professional actress.
I like thick sweaters.
Did I mention I'm new?

Headshots, Getting in the Union, and Building Your Résumé 41

I'd like to remind you that this is the headshot of a person who fully believed she was going to be a rich and famous actor within six months of living in LA. Uh, okay, Jenna.

In case you are wondering, I'm twenty-one years old in this headshot. It was taken by the tech professor in my college theater department, Ron Rybkowski. He was an awesome teacher and every year he would take headshots for any juniors or seniors that wanted them—for free. He hung a backdrop with nice lighting and took a few simple photos of each student.

I used this headshot when I auditioned for summer stock theater. I used it to get meetings with commercial casting agents when I first arrived in Los Angeles. And I used it to submit myself for student films. For a free headshot, that's not too bad. But I quickly realized it was not the best advertisement for my business. I had to get new ones.

So I got this:

Wow.

So, what did I learn? The word *nothing* comes to mind. In many ways, this photo was a step backward. I used a professional headshot photographer, but I refused to listen to any of her advice. Of the hundreds of photos we took that day, I insisted this was the one. Even though the photographer told me it wasn't her favorite, I was certain that this was *the* headshot. Me, clutching my knees, in a pair of overalls covering my whole body. This is a very good example of why *you* should not pick your headshot photo.

Here is a list of people who should *not* help pick your headshot photo:

You
Your husband/boyfriend/girlfriend/wife
Your best friend
Your mom/dad/sister/brother

You shouldn't pick it because you will not be able to put vanity aside, and all those other people will not be able to see you as a sellable commodity.

The following are people who *should* help you to help pick a headshot photo:

The photographer
Teachers
Friends who aren't your best friend
Fellow acting students
Industry professionals such as a casting director, agent, or producer
People at your day job
Strangers

Headshots, Getting in the Union, and Building Your Résumé   43

Let them tell you what your best headshot is, and trust it. Just don't pick it yourself. You can't be objective.

Moving on. After realizing the overalls weren't working, I got this headshot:

What is this? What is happening? Why am I perched on a stool like that? Why is my sweater tucked into my jeans?

I should say, in my defense, I did not send this out. But I did print it. I felt so strongly about it that I had it printed as an option. You see, back when I was starting out, headshots were shot on film and you got contact sheets full of the hundreds of shots from your session. You had to look at them with a little magnifying scope because they were printed really tiny. If you wanted a larger version, you had to pay $10 per 8 × 10 to blow them up. Because money was tight, I typically chose three or four of my favorites from the contact sheet to be blown up. And then I showed these full-size versions to everyone I knew and got their opinion as to which one should become my new headshot. Now do you see why you shouldn't pick your own headshots? I wasted $10 because I wanted to see the stool photo full size. Thank God I had friends to talk me out of it.

Time passed and nothing happened. My hair was getting longer, I wanted to shake things up, so I decided to get a new headshot. I scheduled a session. And I got this:

Headshots, Getting in the Union, and Building Your Résumé

This is not a joke. I am wearing literally the same outfit and sitting in the same closed-off way as my last headshot. To fully appreciate the insanity of this decision I think you need to see them side by side:

Why was I so attached to those overalls? Do I still have them? I'm afraid if I go look in my closet, I may still have them. As you can see, there is absolutely nothing strategic going on in these photos. It's just me, in what is clearly my favorite outfit, smiling.

This brings me to a very interesting part of my history with headshots. Using this overalls headshot, somehow I got an agent. I don't know how or why. In spite of my refusal to wear anything remotely flattering while posing for headshots, I got an agent. (Again, more about this in chapter three.) Guess what? He didn't love my headshot. Upon signing me, he insisted I get new ones. He suggested I use a popular photographer who was known for providing professional styling and makeup on his shoots.

So, I took his advice. And I got this:

I loved this photo. I still love this photo. It makes me look feisty, fierce, powerful, and even sexy. I'd never had anyone capture me in a photo like this before. I loved this idea of me. I got a lot of auditions with this headshot. But what I didn't get was a lot of jobs. And to know why, we must go back to Mara Casey's advice, knowing what you're selling. Clearly, I didn't know. I'm not this girl. I got a lot of auditions followed by a lot of rejection and disappointment. I wasn't getting called in for the roles that I was really right for because my headshot communicated "fierce, sexy girl," and I walked in wearing my ridiculous overalls. You might be thinking, "Burn the damn overalls already! Wear something sexy to the audition!" But remember, I hired professional hair and makeup for this photo shoot. There was

Headshots, Getting in the Union, and Building Your Résumé   47

no way I could recreate that look/mood/feeling on my own, not in my Mazda after a day of transcribing medical jargon. By the way, I'm not against using makeup artists for photo shoots. I actually think it's a good idea. There are ways they can apply makeup that looks natural but also makes your eyes pop or evens out your skin tone. It just has to be subtle.

While my agent loved that sexy shot, my manager suggested I do a re-shoot. We searched for a photographer that specialized in photographing comedic actors. But instead of just booking a session, I decided to finally think critically about my headshot and figure out what I'm selling. After a lot of consideration, I came up with my five adjectives: sweet, trustworthy, open, cute, and vulnerable. I was able to communicate these to the photographer before the shoot.

And that's when I got this shot:

© Susan Maljan

Finally! I did it. I figured out what I was selling! Once again, my five adjectives were: sweet, trustworthy, open, cute, and vulnerable. (I'm not sure you quite get vulnerable out of this picture, but I think I hit the other ones pretty well.) And the shot focused on my face and eyes. No more silly overalls. No more corny poses. This is the headshot that got me called into my audition for Pam on *The Office*. Which makes sense, because this is how the casting notice described the character:

> PAM BEESLY (26-29)—Pam is the receptionist and Jim's friend. Pam is decent, reasonable, and friendly. She has the manner of a nice kindergarten teacher or a future mom. She is an ordinary woman with a sense of humor. She allows her loutish boss to push her around some, but can exhibit flashes of working-class toughness in protecting her friends. She's not cynical or a smartass, although her way of disagreeing is a gentle sarcasm. She's not arrogant or glamorous or overtly sexy, but she is cute compared to the other office workers, and she loves to play with Jim, who understands her better than Roy, her fiancé. They have become true friends, and their flirting is more serious than they acknowledge. Pam needs to be soft and kind and vulnerable. Pam is the romantic lead.

The adjectives used to describe Pam were decent, friendly, soft, cute, kind, and vulnerable. Can you imagine what would have happened if my agent had sent my old headshot? The one with the Angelina Jolie pout and heavy eyeliner? I may have never been called to audition.

Recently I was talking with Allison Jones, the casting director from *The Office*. I told her I was writing a book on the acting business and was currently working on a section about headshots. She said, "Oh Jenna! I still remember your headshot from when you came in for *The Office*. It was so good! It was so you. So Pam!"

Now, that's a good headshot! Over a decade later and she still remembers it. And that's another thing to keep in mind: Not only does your headshot need to get you in the door, it's also what's left behind so they can remember you.

Headshots, Getting in the Union, and Building Your Résumé

Headshot Adjective List:

ADORABLE	FEARFUL	SCARY
ADVENTUROUS	FORGIVING	SCHOLARLY
AFFLUENT	FUN-LOVING	SCRAPPY
AGGRESSIVE	FUNNY	SELF-ASSURED
ANGRY	HANDSOME	SELF-CONSCIOUS
ATHLETIC	HIGH-	SENSITIVE
ATTRACTIVE	MAINTENANCE	SEXY
AUTHORITATIVE	IMPATIENT	SHELTERED
BEAUTIFUL	INNOCENT	SHY
BLUE-COLLAR	INTIMIDATING	SKETCHY
BORED	JOYFUL	SLICK
BOSSY	KIND	SLOPPY
CALM	LAZY	SLY
CARING	LOVING	SMART
CHARACTERY	MEEK	SOULFUL
CHARMING	MELLOW	SPOILED
CLOSED OFF	MISCHIEVOUS	STREET-WISE
COLD	MYSTERIOUS	STRONG
COMBATIVE	NAÏVE	STUDIOUS
COMPETITIVE	NO-NONSENSE	SWEET
COMPLICATED	OLD SOUL	THREATENING
CONFIDENT	OPEN	TOUGH
CONTROLLING	OVERBEARING	TROUBLED
CRANKY	PASSIVE	TRUSTWORTHY
CRAZY	PATIENT	UNASSUMING
CREEPY	PRETTY	UNCOMFORTABLE
DAMAGED	PRUDISH	UNEDUCATED
DANGEROUS	QUIRKY	UNSTABLE
DISTINGUISHED	RUGGED	VULNERABLE
EAGER	SAD	WARM
EDUCATED	SARCASTIC	WHITE-COLLAR
ENERGETIC	SASSY	WISE
ENTITLED	SCARED	

I recommend getting your headshots once you've arrived in New York, Los Angeles, or Chicago, as photographers living in these cities will know current industry standards. For example, when I was starting out, the industry standard was black and white. Every actor had black and white headshots—except for redheads. Isn't that funny? If you were a redhead, you needed a color headshot to show off your red hair. These days everyone is expected to have a color headshot. Sorry, redheads—you don't get to corner the market anymore.

In general, at the time of this book's publication, the going rate for a good Los Angeles or Chicago headshot photographer is around $400 to $650. This rate includes two to three different "looks" plus two to three retouched final images. The rate in New York is a little higher, around $500 to $875. This doesn't include the cost of a professional makeup artist or the printing of your photos, which combined will run you another $200 to $300. I know, it's not cheap, especially when you're struggling.

As you can clearly see, I didn't get it right the first time. Or the second. Or even the third. And it will probably take you a few sessions to figure out how to get the best photo as well. Very few people end up loving their first headshots. After all, we aren't models. I managed to get an agent and work, even with my less-than-ideal headshots. So don't freak out if you feel like you aren't mastering it right away. All you need is one decent photo to get you started. So, make the best of your session, use the five adjectives, and try to have some fun.

STEP TWO: GETTING IN THE UNION

When an actor tells you the story of how they got their SAG-AFTRA card, it usually starts with a deep sigh, followed by a long, drawn-out story that sounds almost as exciting as a trip to the dentist. This is because you cannot get a professional acting job unless you are in the

Headshots, Getting in the Union, and Building Your Résumé

union, but you cannot get into the union unless you have a professional acting job. A textbook catch-22. It took me three years to get my union card. And I consider my journey one of the easier ones.

The two most popular ways to get into SAG-AFTRA are performing in television commercials or doing extra work. First, let's discuss commercials.

Commercials

If you book a union commercial job, you gain access to the union. Instantly. Boom. You're in. Because unlike film and television work, you don't need to be a member of SAG-AFTRA to book a role in a union commercial. You also don't need much experience, because oftentimes commercials are more about the look of an actor. But what you do need is a commercial agent. You might be thinking, "Hold up, Jenna. At the beginning of this chapter you said I wasn't ready to look for an agent." True, I did say that. But I was referring to a theatrical agent; commercial agents are different. Commercial agents only submit their clients for work in commercials. Like theatrical agents, commercial agents receive 10 percent of whatever you earn from commercial work. These agents usually have higher client lists than theatrical agents, mainly because commercial agents pretty much pack their files with as many fresh, interesting faces as they can find, and then they play the numbers game. This means it's generally easier to find a commercial agent than a theatrical agent. The catch is, you need to find a *good* commercial agent to work with. And this is harder than you might think.

Take, for example, my friend Paul's first experience with a commercial agent. Upon arriving in LA, Paul immediately set out to find a commercial agent. He sent his headshot around town and within a week was signed by an agency. Woohoo! He was thrilled! Did it really matter that the commercial agent opted to meet him at a café, instead of her office? Apparently not to Paul, because he took his buddies to a bar to celebrate. Three cheers for Paul! Drink up! The next morning, or afternoon, he woke up to an epic hangover. He felt awful, like the bottom of a shoe. But the hangover became tolerable when he remembered the good news: He had a commercial agent! He got up and called her. No answer. Hmm. He tried again. The phone seemed to be disconnected. Weird. He decided to drive on over to her office, which turned out to be an apartment. After ringing the doorbell a few dozen times, a neighbor came out and told Paul that his new commercial agent had been evicted. He started the process over and, eventually, he got one with an office.

> "I vowed I would never do a commercial, nor would I do a soap opera—both of which I did as soon as I left the Acting Company and was starving."
> —Kevin Kline

My favorite story involving the search for a good commercial agent comes from my friend Aynsley. Over the course of seven years she has had six different commercial agents. Six! How did she burn through so many agents so quickly? Well, her first agent left the business without telling her. The second one died. The third one never sent her on a single audition. Her fourth agent . . . wait for it . . . died. The fifth agent dropped her because they felt she was "too plain." Ouch. Exhausted from all the rejection, and fed up with the revolving door of agents, Aynsley basically gave up on a career in commercials. But a few years later, a co-worker happened to show Aynsley's materials to a friend who was a successful commercial agent. The agent was taken with Aynsley. She loved that Aynsley had a baby face, was from the Midwest, and was not stick thin. She agreed to represent her. A smart choice, as Aynsley went on to book seven national commercials within the first year of signing. Talk about an exercise in patience that finally paid off big time!

After five months of mass-mailing my smiling headshot to every commercial agent in town, eventually I got signed to a top commercial agency. It felt pretty good to sign with them, like things were falling into place. I was confident I'd book a commercial in no time, and finally get into the union. Well, like almost everything in Hollywood,

Headshots, Getting in the Union, and Building Your Résumé

it's not that easy. Finding a commercial agent is only the first step. After that, you've got to actually book a commercial, which proved to be much more difficult.

I found commercial auditions particularly hard to navigate because they often involved no scripted lines. As a trained actor, I was used to delivering dialogue and playing characters. Commercial auditions seemed to be mostly about improvisation and appearance. One of my first commercial auditions was as "a young frazzled housewife" for a new kitchen floor cleaner. I asked my agent how I should prepare. She told me not to worry, I'd get all the instructions when I arrived at the audition. This is pretty common with commercials; it's rare to receive any materials prior to the day of the audition. I decided to arrive a half hour early so I could look over the materials and practice. I was expecting to see some sort of dialogue sheet about my messy kitchen floor that was magically transformed after using XYZ product. But when I got there, I saw nothing. Only a sign-in sheet next to a little cartoon drawing of the commercial. I signed in and didn't give it much thought. When I went into the room, the casting director asked me to state my name to the camera and then said, "If you could go anywhere in the world, where would you go and why?" (Random. Not sure what that had to do with floor cleaner.) I was upbeat and friendly, "My name is Jenna Fischer. If I could go anywhere in the world, I'd like to go on safari in Africa and pet baby lions." Okay, not the most witty response, but it was the truth. However, clearly the truth wasn't enough, because I didn't get the part. In fact, I never got any part. I went on countless commercial auditions and never booked a single one. Zero. Recently, an acting student told me that she goes on commercial auditions all the time that ask for a "Jenna Fischer Type." Ironic, right? When Jenna Fischer was auditioning for commercials, no one was interested.

To help you, I decided to ask some experienced commercial actors for their advice, since I'm clearly not a master of the commercial audition process. My friends all said the same thing: *Study the storyboards.* A storyboard is a template created by the advertising agency that tells the shot-by-shot story of the commercial. They basically look like a comic strip, and you usually find them hanging on the wall by the sign-in sheet. (Aha! That little cartoon from the floor cleaner audition!) If you take a moment to absorb them, they will explain your role in the spot, as well as the overall energy and tone of the commercial. Advertisers sweat over each word and visual when creating a storyboard, because they only have thirty seconds to sell their product. So storyboards need to be precise. Your job is to really study the storyboard and absorb it, then go into the room and recreate it. Show the advertisers that you're the guy from the storyboard.

Another piece of advice from my expert friends: Next time you're watching television, actually watch the commercials. You'll notice that in most ads, the actors don't say anything at all. Commercials tend to be a series of images with a narrator's voice laid over the top. Sure, sometimes the actors talk, but it's usually just a few words. What's more important is what they're doing and how they look doing it. Understanding this nuance can be really helpful. Because when you're called into the audition room and asked some random question about your favorite vacation spot, it doesn't really matter what you *say*. What matters is that you convey the tone of the commercial. If the commercial is about a frazzled housewife freaking out over her soiled floor, but you present a chipper, upbeat attitude, chances are you're not getting a callback. Don't worry about being likable, unless the commercial asks for likable. You want to convey the energy of the commercial in every aspect of your audition. From the way you enter the room, to the way you introduce yourself, to how you answer questions or say your lines.

After he found a good agent with an actual office, my friend Paul got called to audition for a commercial about car insurance. His audition group had six people, all clumped together in a tiny room. They were told to be angry and annoyed that the insurance company wouldn't open their doors to deal with their questions. Paul was put at the end of the group, next to a particularly obnoxious actor who kept elbowing his way into the shot. Paul was annoyed. He spent the

Pontiac Bantam - "Chaos" (0:30) - Storyboard

OPEN on a woman in her mid-30s hurriedly walking her two elementary-aged kids to school on a busy residential street in the morning.

Quickly, more action happens around them and their pace gets faster. Kids whiz by on bicycles and skateboards. A lawnmower roars. A dog starts barking.

It starts raining on them. While crossing the street, mom accidentally drops her phone and it shatters. The crossing guard shouts as other parents join in.
CROSSING GUARD: Move it, mom!

CUT TO the interior of a minivan as a different mom and her two kids drive to school. All of the previous chaos was just a movie the kids are watching on the foldout TV screen in the backseat.
DAUGHTER: Move it, Mom!
They all laugh.

Mom pulls into the drop-off lane at the elementary school. The kids get out and run into school.

Mom smiles and drives off.
VOICE OVER: The new Bantam from Pontiac. Ready when you are.
CUT TO Pontiac logo.

Illustrated by Jess LaGreca

entire audition pissed off and frustrated by this upstaging buffoon. He left the audition and drove home thinking, "I can't believe I drove all the way to Venice for that." Well, imagine his surprise when he booked the job. Upon talking to the director on the day of the shoot, Paul was told they loved how angry and annoyed he was in his audition, that he conveyed the perfect amount of frustration. Ha! Thanks to the buffoon, Paul didn't have to *act*; he just had to *be*!

Which brings me to the final important piece of advice from the commercial gurus: *You* are not the star of the commercial. The actor's job in a commercial is to be a supporting player for the real star of the spot . . . the product. Just act naturally and don't put on a big show. Be there for the product. And be real. Be a real car buyer confused about mortgage rates, a real father proud of his son's first home run, a real mom diapering her first child. Real, real, real. That's the mantra of commercials.

Extra Work

Have you ever wondered about the people dancing in the background of a wedding reception while Owen Wilson flirts with Rachel McAdams? Or how about the ones running hysterically from a falling meteor behind Tom Cruise? Well, if you haven't, let me enlighten you: Those are called extras. Hollywood couldn't tell stories without them. Pretty much anyone off the street can be an extra. You don't need training, you don't need a headshot, you don't need an agent, and you don't have to be in the union.

In fact, if you do enough work as an extra, you can actually earn your way into the union. That's how I did it. Here's how it works: Big union productions hire both union and non-union extras to work on their projects. If they haven't met their quota of union extras, or if the work requires a special skill that only a non-union person can perform, they will bump up non-union extras to be union extras for

Headshots, Getting in the Union, and Building Your Résumé

the day. When this happens, you receive a union pay rate and, more importantly, you get a voucher. (A voucher is a production "timecard" that verifies your union-level work for the day.) Once you've earned three vouchers, you become eligible to join the union. But before you get too excited, keep in mind that you will most likely have to work many non-union jobs before you're lucky enough to be bumped up.

If you're curious about how a set works, being an extra is a great way to observe the action. However, I should warn you, there are a few downsides to being an extra. It's not, uh, glamorous. In fact, it's pretty grueling. Unless you enjoy being packed into a makeshift tent with no heat or air conditioning, waiting with dozens of other people as they light the set and rehearse with the actors. Also, there are never enough chairs for everyone, so perhaps you'll find it fun to sit on the ground. But to be honest, it hardly matters because the chairs are cheap and uncomfortable anyway. The restroom is usually a Porta-potty (yay, ladies!), and if they do offer you food, it's most likely something bought in bulk at Costco. (Tip: Pack your own snacks, water, and lunch. And bring a book, because there is probably no WiFi.)

I got my first job as an extra on my third day in Los Angeles. I was so excited. I had barely unpacked and I already had a job! A friend of mine from college worked at Central Casting and heard about a commercial shoot for a new ride at Universal Studios in which non-union extras would earn $100 for the day because it required some "stunts." Whatever that meant, we didn't know. We didn't care! This was double the usual non-union rate, so we jumped at the chance. We heard rumors that we might even earn a voucher. Everything about the job seemed amazing. It was at Universal Studios and we were given special passes to drive onto the lot and park. This was particularly exciting because I had never been on a studio lot before. As we walked from our car to the shoot location, we passed by a variety of old movie sets, including the downtown street used in *Back to the Future*. I couldn't believe it. I was walking past the clock tower! And then we saw Arnold Schwarzenegger playing basketball outside one of the sound stages.

Are you kidding me? I had only been in town three days and I was already on a studio lot, practically hanging out with the Terminator! My friend and I were giddy and excited. We couldn't stop laughing and talking about our great luck.

When we got to the set, we learned that the shoot was a commercial for a new roller coaster water ride based on the movie *Jurassic Park*. We were loaded into a little boat and told where to look and when to scream. The boat took off, and we laughed and screamed as we sped through the water, passing all sorts of giant dinosaurs. Then at the end of the ride, the boat climbed up a giant hill and careened down at breakneck speed, ending in a giant splash. It was really fun. We laughed and smiled as the little boat glided through the water and the ride started again. Laugh! Point! Scream! Even the second time was fun. Again, after it was over, we laughed and smiled as the little boat glided though the water and the ride started again. And, again after that. And, again after that. We rode the Jurassic water ride for twelve hours.

> "Dreaming about being an actress is more exciting than being one."
> —Marilyn Monroe

Let me say that again: We rode the Jurassic water ride for *twelve hours*. But that's not all. To make the ride seem more dramatic, they had men with hoses spraying us with water along the way. Warm water? Nope. The water was freezing cold. This went on and on, until we were all very sad. And then, at the end of the day, just when we thought it couldn't get any worse, they brought out the "water cannon." Apparently they needed close-ups. So, they shot the water cannon over and over again, pelting each of us as we cowered in fear. (Real fear. We weren't pretending anymore. The water cannon was as terrifying as a real dinosaur.) The man sitting next to me started crying a little to himself. I think he'd been getting the worst of the water cannon. I realized this because on the very next shot, just as the water cannon boomed, he leaned far back in his seat. As a result, I got blasted in the face with a giant, icy-cold water cannonball. It hurt. It was torture. Seriously, the

Headshots, Getting in the Union, and Building Your Résumé   59

CIA should consider the Jurassic method because, by the end, I was ready to name names, any name, to get me off that damn ride.

My friend and I barely spoke as we walked back to our car after the shoot. We were soaking wet, starving, and completely shell-shocked. We didn't earn a SAG voucher, and we'd only made $100. Even now, when my family comes to town and wants to go to Universal Studios, I can't ride that ride. Last time I checked, they still play parts of the commercial as you stand in line for the ride. If you pause it juuuuuust right, you can see half of my wet face screaming at a dinosaur.

My best experience as an extra was in a commercial for a new long-distance phone service. It was a big-budget commercial, and I was playing a member of a field hockey team. The shoot was about two hours' drive out of town, which meant we got to stay in a hotel overnight—all expenses paid. It felt like a mini paid vacation! And the shoot was simple. While the lead girl talked about long distance, I stood in the background with other girls, pretending we were at field hockey practice. It was perfect. I was well fed. I liked the other girls. I made something like $1,200 in two days—and I got a voucher toward being in the union. It was a long way from Jurassic disaster.

After countless other crappy background assignments, I finally got my additional vouchers working as an extra in the movie *Pleasantville* starring Reese Witherspoon and Tobey Maguire. I got a call from Central Casting saying that they needed people with a certain "look" described as "innocent, 1950s, teenager" for a two-week job. They wanted people over eighteen to look young so that they didn't have to pay for chaperones and tutors or work child hours (which are shorter than a normal workday). Well, you've seen my first headshot, I could definitely play "under eighteen." I was told there was a good chance I could earn vouchers on this project, but to choose me, they would need to see me in person. The set was in the desert, about an hour outside of Los Angeles. I didn't care, I needed those vouchers! I drove my hot car with the broken air conditioner straight into the desert. Lucky for me, I looked young enough. I got to go through full

The Actor's Life

Me, on the set of Pleasantville, *1997*

hair, makeup, and wardrobe, and be transformed into a 1950s malt shop teen. It was so fun. I felt like a real working actor.

Of the ten days I worked on the project, I think I was only called to the set three times. Twice for a malt shop scene and once to stand on the street. But both times I got to see Reese Witherspoon and Tobey Maguire working. It was so cool! The best part of the *Pleasantville* job was that by the end of the shoot, I had finally earned the additional vouchers I needed to join SAG. I was now a union gal.

HOW TO FIND WORK AS AN EXTRA

So, how do you sign up to be an extra? The top extras casting agency is Central Casting. Registration is free, and

Headshots, Getting in the Union, and Building Your Résumé

productions are always looking for new people. Central Casting has offices in New York, Los Angeles, Atlanta, and New Orleans. The process for registering is easy. Simply visit a Central Casting office, where you will be photographed and asked to fill out a W-4 form. I would suggest arriving early. The registration lines are long, and they only accept a certain amount of people per day. If you don't make it in the room, you have to come back the next day and start all over again.

There are no auditions for background work. Once registered, you call a hotline each morning to see if there's work that matches your type. You must call early; the jobs are first come, first serve.

Central Casting offers several workshops about extra work taught by industry professionals. If you are new to the business, take these workshops. They are *free* and will teach you what to expect as a background performer. They also explain the voucher system and pay structure for non-union and union extra work.

A brief note about scams: Yes, they do happen, so be alert. There are two primary ways that people try to scam new actors looking for work as an extra.

SCAM ALERT #1: A real voucher *cannot* be purchased. Anyone claiming they can sell you a SAG-AFTRA voucher is a scam artist. You must have a timecard with *your* name on it. When you receive a voucher, you will always also receive a paystub—this is how SAG-AFTRA knows it is legit.

SCAM ALERT #2: Beware of companies claiming to provide you with extra work for a monthly fee. This monthly fee is called "fee for services," and it is not likely to get you work. Many such companies target people

> *(... Continued)*
> living outside New York and Los Angeles. A legitimate casting service does not charge for finding people work. They get paid by the studio, not by you.

Taft-Hartley

A very rare way to gain access to the SAG-AFTRA union is a little loophole called Taft-Hartley. If you are lucky enough to gain access to an audition for a speaking role on a union film or television show, and if you beat out all of the union actors for the job, the production company can submit a Taft-Hartley form to SAG-AFTRA, requesting your immediate inclusion in the union. You pay your dues, and you're in. In my experience, getting a Taft-Hartley is as rare as winning the lottery. Most of the time it is used for instances where a very specific set of attributes are needed (six foot tall, blonde female who speaks fluent Japanese, for example) that simply cannot be filled by a union actor. In my twenty years of being in Los Angeles, I only know one person who ever got a Taft-Hartley into the union. But that is changing due to a little something called the Web Series.

Web Series

The newest way to gain membership in the union is to get cast in (i.e., create your own) new media show, or web series. Creating a union-eligible web series might sound like a major undertaking, but it could be worth the trouble.

To become eligible, your project must have three things: a script, a budget, and at least one current and qualified SAG-AFTRA cast member. You will be required to fill out a bunch of forms, all of which can be found at www.sag.org. If SAG approves your preliminary form, you will be sent a Station 12 form, which asks you to list all of the performers in your project, both union and non-union. It is at this time that you, as the producer, can request a Taft-Hartley for you, the actor, and get yourself into the union. Pretty sneaky, right? The kicker is that you actually have to film the series and post the results. But, that's a good thing, right? I know people who have done this with budgets as low as $300. However, a more realistic budget would probably land in the $1,000 to $5,000 range. You will need to feed your crew, purchase props and costumes, and most likely rent a small lighting package or camera. You'll also have to pay your union actors. Remember, you are going to have to post this on the internet. It will be the beginning of your body of work. You want it to be good.

When it comes to getting in the union, you just have to try anything and everything you can to get in. Don't get discouraged. Everyone has a different story, a different path. You may end up riding a theme park ride in hopes of earning a voucher, or perhaps you book a commercial. It's not a perfect science, so you should try every angle.

BECOMING "SAG-AFTRA ELIGIBLE"

After you've collected three vouchers, been given a Taft-Hartley, or once you've been cast in a union commercial, you will become "SAG-AFTRA Eligible." This means you're qualified to join the union at any time. However, before you rush your checkbook down to the SAG-AFTRA office, you might want to check the financial commitment. The current rate to join SAG-AFTRA is $3,000. After paying the initial fee, you are required to pay an annual base fee of $206, plus "work dues," which is 1.575 percent of your SAG earnings. Also, once you join the union, you are not allowed to work non-union jobs anymore. This includes some web series and internet content, so be careful. You can be fined, or even thrown out of the union, if you're caught working on projects outside of the union's jurisdiction.

My advice is to reap the benefits of being "SAG-AFTRA Eligible." During this transitional time, you are allowed to pursue both union and non-union work—which is important for building your résumé. When I was in this position, I created two résumés: one that said I was SAG-AFTRA and one that said I was non-union, both of which were essentially true. Being in this unique situation, I was able to submit myself for all kinds of work. After securing a few more non-union roles, I eventually booked a two-line role in a union film starring Rob Lowe. I raced down to the SAG-AFTRA offices and paid my initiation fee.

Joining the unions is expensive. But in return, members gain access to professional work, better pay through salary requirements, residual payments, pension and health coverage, and protection from abusive work conditions.

STEP THREE: GAIN EXPERIENCE AND BUILD YOUR RÉSUMÉ

Let's say you've taken my advice. You've trained, acquired great headshots, and are working to get in the union. There's only one more detail to work on: your résumé. Ideally, you want your résumé to communicate two things: experience and training. Training is easy enough to get on your own. Experience is a lot harder.

When you're first starting out, your experience will be somewhat limited, so you'll need to get creative in order to build your résumé. Forget about studio films and network television—those will come down the road. Right now focus on student films, short films, independent features, web shows, and industrial films (if you've ever worked in fast food and been made to watch a video about how to use the fryer, that's an industrial film)—basically, anything that puts you in front of a camera doing acting work. You've got to hustle. And by the way, get used to hustling, because here's a dirty secret about the business that no one ever tells you: Even after you get an agent, you still have to hustle. In fact, even after you've been on an iconic television show for nine years, you *still* have to hustle. It's very rare to get into the position where the work continually flows to you.

Speaking of hustling, here is a copy of my first résumé. This is what I attached to the photo taken by my theater professor:

Jenna Fischer

Height: 5'6"
Weight: 117

Vocal Range: Alto

Stage Experience:

Noises Off!	Poppy	NMSU* Mainstage
Boys Next Door	Sheila	H&A** Theatre
Cabaret	Kit Kat Kitten	The Studio Theatre
West Side Story	Velma	H&A Theatre
Murder at the Haunted Mansion!	Abby/Cassie	Upstage Productions

Television and Film Experience:

Truman	Farming Extra	HBO Pictures
Clea & Toby	Clea	NE-TV
SEX	Elizabeth Story	NMSU Film Festival
Kirksville 63501	Gabrielle	NEMO News
Commercial	Waitress	KTVO/ABC

Special Talents & Awards:

- Choreography with over 10 years dance experience in all areas. Shows include: *Cabaret, The Mikado, Boys Next Door, & Godspell.*
- Silver Medal winner for ballet at Young American's National Invitational Dance Competition in Anaheim, CA.
- Nominated Best Supporting Actress in a film at NMSU annual Film Festival.
- Member of Alpha Psi Omega, National Honorary Dramatics Fraternity.

As you can see, this is not the résumé of a person who is ready to be a series regular on a TV show. It's the résumé of a person who needs to hustle. Yes, it shows I'm trained and that I'm serious about a career in acting. But it also shows that I'm not in the union and that I have no real professional acting experience. All of my credits are from doing college theater or college television.

If you had several million dollars to finance a movie, who would you to hire to star in it? A union actor with years of experience, or the person with this résumé? I think the answer is clear. It doesn't matter how much raw talent I possessed. Based on this résumé, chances are I'm not ready. Even the best actors need seasoning and time to grow into their potential. View this period as your time to grow and gain experience. Get out there and start getting any work you can. That's exactly what I did. The more I worked, the better I became.

Self-Submissions

> "If you don't drive your business, you will be driven out of business."
> —B. C. Forbes

When I was starting out, the only option for getting non-union auditions was through the classifieds in the back of a periodical called *Backstage*. *Backstage* was a printed magazine that came out every Thursday. Every week, I'd go to the newsstand, buy the latest copy, and carefully read the audition notices, circling anything I felt I was remotely right for. My kitchen table was transformed into a small mail center with stacks of headshots, résumés, and envelopes ready to be addressed. I loved Thursday. Thursday was a day filled with hope and optimism. It was the day I might read the listing that, I believed, would change my life.

It was through these submissions that I got my very first paid, on-camera acting job in Los Angeles. Was it a role in a Martin Scorsese film? Uh, no. It was a role in a sex education video for mental patients

Headshots, Getting in the Union, and Building Your Résumé 67

upon their release from UCLA Medical Center. Yep, you read that right. Imagine me at Thanksgiving, telling my family about that career milestone. It paid $100, and I was promised a copy of the industrial when it was completed. It was a two-part video. One portion of the video explained exactly how to have sex. I wasn't in that part. No, my job was in the second part of the video, explaining how to use contraceptives. I played a girl who was going on a date and, while I'm getting ready, my older sister came in the bathroom and said something like, "Wow, you're spending a lot of time getting ready. You must really like this one." And I said, "Oh yes, I really like him," and she said, "Well, are you bringing protection?" and I said, "Protection? Protection from what?" (That was my favorite line.) She said, "Well, if you decide to become sexually active, you need protection from pregnancy and sexually transmitted diseases." She opened up our bathroom drawer, presumably a drawer I'd never bothered to open, and inside was every contraceptive imaginable. This included an IUD, which actually has to be implanted by a gynecologist. But, for some reason, we had an IUD in our magic bathroom drawer. She held up the items one by one and described how they work. My job was to sit and listen very earnestly and then say, "Thanks, Sis! I'm glad I know how to protect myself," and go off to my date.

And that was my very first professional acting job, all shot in one day. I wore my own clothes and did my own makeup. But listen, beggars can't be choosers. It was not the time to be picky. I needed credits and this was a credit. Even better, it was real on-camera experience with a lot of dialogue. Everyone has to start somewhere. How funny that my start was with the line, "Protection? Protection from what?"

From there, I concentrated on submitting myself for student films and non-union independent movies. Within a few months, I booked two different non-union feature films from submissions I made through *Backstage*. One was a crazy comedy about a dysfunctional family called *Channel 493*. I had a supporting role as the sassy daughter. The other was a teen love story called *Born Champion*, basically the same plot as *The Karate Kid*, except instead of karate he did motocross. I earned zero dollars for *Channel 493* and about $300 for *Born Champion*. Both jobs were totally awesome. In both cases, I got to create a character and do multiple scenes. And, like the sex education video, I wore my own clothes and did my own makeup.

The best part about these jobs was what they taught me about the process of making a feature film. I learned that movies don't typically shoot in chronological order. For example, we shot the final scene from *Born Champion* on the first day. On the second day, we shot the flirting scenes. I still barely knew the guy. It was literally like, "Hello, nice to meet you. Let's go stand over by those motorcycles and flirt." This was a whole new challenge for me, acting-wise. I was used to doing plays where you rehearsed and performed things in story order. I had to figure out how to express a comfort level and chemistry for the flirting scene, which I then had to undo three days later when we shot the scene where we awkwardly meet at school for the first time. So crazy. Luckily, almost everyone else on the project was new too. We were all learning together.

The same was true of *Channel 493*. I enjoyed that one so much that I still have the prop I stole from the movie in my office. Neither film got me any closer to getting in the union. But, they both got finished and I gained valuable experience. Not to mention, I had a lot of fun, met cool people, earned two great credits for my résumé and scenes for my demo reel.

Demo Reels

What is a demo reel? A demo reel is a professionally produced collection of scenes that highlight an actor's best work in various films, television shows, or web series. If a headshot is considered the packaging, a demo reel is the commercial.

Headshots, Getting in the Union, and Building Your Résumé

> Every actor needs a demo reel. They can be an invaluable resource, both before and after you find an agent. When creating yours, be strategic. It should be around three minutes in length, showcasing your most compelling work. Keep in mind, a demo reel is not a video you shoot at home, or in an acting class. It is also not a montage of your work set to music. It should consist of professionally produced work and be updated when necessary. At the very least, you want it to show agents and casting directors that you have experience in front of the camera. At the very best, you want it to show range and talent and to be entertaining.
>
> Casting websites allow you to upload a link to your demo reel. You can also link your reel to sites like YouTube or Vimeo. If you only have one scene on your demo reel at first, that's okay. Everyone has to start somewhere.

Gone are the days of buying stamps and mailing audition submissions. Today we have the internet. No more post office. No more waiting by the phone. You can sign up for casting websites, create a profile with your headshot and résumé, scan the casting notices (which are updated daily, even hourly), digitally submit yourself for work, and usually get a response within twenty-four hours. So much easier!

Most casting websites require you to pay a monthly fee for their service, while some provide job listings at no cost. As with most things in life, you get what you pay for. The sites that require a fee typically have access to the most auditions. I would normally warn you about places that charge you a fee, but these are legit businesses.

Casting Websites: What You Need to Know

LA Casting and NY Casting

LA Casting (www.lacasting.com) and **NY Casting** (www.nycasting.com) are the big dogs on the block, casting student films, independent features, and music videos. The company's websites are great resources for people looking to build their résumés and gain on-camera experience. At the time of publication, the basic package costs $14.95 a month and includes a personal profile page with one photo, unlimited updates to your résumé, a personal URL to your page that you can send to agents or casting directors on your own, plus access to the Casting Billboard, which posts new jobs daily. You can submit yourself for work and even upload a demo reel when you have one. If you want to add more photos, that will cost more money. But this website is a great place to start.

Other similar sites are **Casting Frontier** and **The People Network** (TPN). You might want to look into them as well. *Backstage* still publishes casting notices every Thursday. But now you're able to sign up at Backstage.com and submit yourself digitally.

Before you sign up, it's important to know that you must live in New York or Los Angeles to participate in the respective casting sites. These websites advertise for jobs that are happening right now, not in two months. For example, a friend of mine just submitted herself for a digital short on a Wednesday, auditioned on Thursday, got the job, and shot on Saturday. It is a waste of money to

Headshots, Getting in the Union, and Building Your Résumé   71

sign up for casting websites if you aren't in a position to actually audition for and work the jobs. If you are hoping to gain experience or build your résumé before moving to Los Angeles or New York, check the local film commission websites in your city. They often list casting notices for local filming. If you are looking for New York stage auditions, your best resources are **Playbill.com**, *Backstage*'s **Blogstage** website, or the **Actors' Equity** website.

Actors Access

Owned by Breakdown Services, **Actors Access** is the big website for union film and television casting. Eventually every serious actor winds up with a profile on Actors Access. Your profile is linked with your theatrical agent and, through the site, they are able to submit you for work using your profile page. The non-union postings this site provides are mostly for student films and independent features. Sometimes, casting directors open up union jobs to actors for self-submission. It's rare, but it happens. You can probably wait to sign up for Actors Access until after you are in the union and have an agent. It is more of a tool for your theatrical agent to make submissions than a tool for self-submissions. Membership costs $68 per year, with extra fees for uploading videos and other media. Also, a little tip: Actors with video on their profiles appear at the top of the pile in submissions, so it's imperative to have a "full" profile on Actors Access.

Continued . . .

IMDbPro

You might already be familiar with the popular film and television search site **Internet Movie Database** (or IMDb, for short). Every film or television show ever made, or currently in development or production, has a page that lists the full cast and crew, budget, and release details. Directors, actors, writers, producers, and other crew members have individual pages that list their credits. If you thought to yourself, "Hey, I'd like to watch every movie Cate Blanchett has ever made," this is the place to go for a list of where you should start. But there is also a more substantial version of the site used by industry professionals called **IMDbPro**. Once you start booking jobs in professional film and television projects, you will want to sign up for IMDbPro and manage your profile, which is usually automatically created for you once you are cast in a big union project. But adding a photo and managing the page are your responsibilities and require a fee. While you are not able to submit yourself for work using IMDbPro, casting directors and producers often use this site to quickly get an idea of an actor's résumé, job history, and current look. As a producer, I've used the site myself. I was putting together a pitch for a new television show and wanted to suggest a certain actor for the lead role. I was able to use the site to see if the actor was already committed to any projects that would make them unavailable, which was important to know before suggesting them to the network.

Headshots, Getting in the Union, and Building Your Résumé

Don't Accidentally Become a Sex Worker

When you're submitting yourself for auditions, you've got to be a little careful when sizing up which jobs are legitimate. For the most part, the auditions on professional casting sites can be trusted. But I definitely do *not* recommend applying for jobs you find on Craigslist or the classified section of newspapers, as they have not been vetted in any way whatsoever. You don't want to find yourself in a sketchy situation, like the time I accidentally almost joined a high-priced call girl ring.

It all started when a friend of mine found a listing for an open call in the back of a free LA newspaper. Auditions were being held to find the fifth member of an all-girls singing group that was being billed as the *International Spice Girls*. (Because that's how international singing groups are put together . . . through advertisements in the back of a free weekly paper. This should have been RED FLAG #1.)

In case you're too young to remember, the Spice Girls were a British all-girl singing group sensation, the female version of One Direction or Backstreet Boys. And they were *huge*. Victoria Beckham was a Spice Girl.

My friend was a singer. She knew I didn't sing, but she asked if I'd come along and keep her company. I had nothing better to do, so I agreed. And just for fun, I decided to audition as well. We hopped in the car and found ourselves driving to an apartment complex deep in Van Nuys. This seemed a little strange, but when we arrived, there was a long line of singers waiting to audition, so the whole thing felt legitimate. (Looking back, an audition at an apartment complex should have been RED FLAG #2.)

We waited for more than an hour, and when I finally got my chance, I sang Nancy Sinatra's "These Boots Are Made for Walkin'." I knew the song very well—I'd sung it in my car hundreds of times. But more importantly, it has about three notes, all in the mid-C range. A simple song was essential for me because I am a terrible singer. I'm not tone-deaf, but I am tone-challenged. For example, when I played Darlene Madison in the movie *Walk Hard*, a role that required great singing, my voice was dubbed over by a professional singer. I remember the day the director gently took me aside and said, "You know, Jenna, we hired you for your acting, you're a very good actress. You are not, however, such a great singer. Sooooo . . . we've decided to dub your voice." Or perhaps you remember the "Grief Counseling" episode of *The Office*, the one where Pam sings "On the Wings of Love" at the bird funeral? I'm not trying to be funny in that scene. That's my best effort.

So, anyway, given my lackluster singing talent, imagine my surprise when I received a phone call saying I was cast as the fifth International Spice Girl! I was shocked. *Me? Bad Singer Jenna?* (This should have been RED FLAG #3.)

When I spoke with the producer of the group, he was very excited. He said he loved my wholesome look. His plan was to sell me as a sweet country girl, very Americana and straight off the farm. He told me to come by the next day and pick up a tape of their music, so I could start learning the songs.

Less than a week later he called to say they were already gearing up to go on tour. He assured me I would be ready and invited me to his condo for some coaching. (RED FLAG #4!) In the days since, I've come to learn that when you meet with legitimate producers, managers, or directors, they don't hold auditions or have meetings in their homes. But I didn't know that then. I was new and fresh off the bus (and didn't have a book like this to warn me!).

I arrived for my work session, which actually wasn't in the dumpy Van Nuys apartment, but a very nice penthouse condominium. Once inside, to my relief, I noticed that there were many other girls there. However (RED FLAG #5), they were all walking around in some form of lingerie. Nothing too revealing—silk robes and negligees. The producer guy would occasionally point to someone and say, "Oh, there's Svetlana; she's our Russian girl," and I would sort of wave at Svetlana, who would wave back, confused.

Headshots, Getting in the Union, and Building Your Résumé

The producer and I settled in the living room to work on my song, a little ditty about a girl at a truck stop. I danced around and sang the tune, doing my best to stay on pitch. After a while, he sat me down to talk about my future. He said I had real potential and he wanted to manage my acting career. He seemed very focused on the fact that I needed new headshots. In particular, nude headshots (GIANT HUGE RED FLAG!). He then graciously offered to take the photos himself. "So that you will be most comfortable," he said. Wow. What a guy. He went on to explain that I might find myself on an audition where nudity was required. What would I do? I wouldn't want to have to get naked in the casting director's office, would I? Instead, I'd be able to show off my brand-new nude photographs. Problem solved! (Side note: Legitimate casting directors *never* ask you to take off your clothes in their office. You probably knew that, but I felt like it was worth mentioning, just in case some creep tries to convince you otherwise.)

I was starting to get suspicious. (Duh!) I mean, in addition to the lingerie girls and the nude photograph offer, no one else was doing any singing or dancing. I was the only one practicing. Just little old me, singing my heart out about that truck stop, while lingerie-clad women strolled through the condo. What's going on here?!

At this point, probably sensing my discomfort, the producer said to me, "Okay, you're great, the song is great, you have your first show this Friday." I was a little shocked, I still hadn't rehearsed with the other girls or learned my choreography. He told me not to worry—this was a solo show for "a small group of traveling Japanese businessmen." (Which is so cliché, I'm embarrassed to even be writing it!) He went on, "After the show it would be very nice if you provided these gentlemen with some companionship. You only have to do as much as you want. But some of the girls have found this to be an easy way to make extra income." And *that* was when I finally realized the truth about the International Spice Girls: It was a cover for a call-girl operation—a very classy, high-priced call-girl operation.

I was totally freaking out. I tried to act natural and nodded along, while quietly plotting my exit. "Wow, that sounds interesting. Very interesting. I love Japan," I said, cheerfully, as I pretended to search for my organizer. "Hmm. It must be in my car; I'll be right back," I said as I walked toward the door. I ran out of the building and promptly went home, changed my number, and dropped off the face of the planet. Thankfully, the creepy "producer" didn't know where I lived. He only had my disconnected phone number.

You might be wondering, "What took you so long to figure this out?" I ask myself the same thing. All I can conclude is that I had been so blinded by my ambition that I wasn't paying attention to a potentially dangerous situation. And also, the truck stop song was really good.

Bear in mind, this is not just a cautionary tale for the ladies. I have a male friend who accidentally accepted a role in a soft-core porn film. When he auditioned for the film, the description of the project was vague. There was nothing in the audition that indicated he would be expected to strip naked and perform elaborate simulated sex scenes. He got the role and was very excited. But then something seemed off. His phone calls with the production company were weird, and he grew suspicious when they couldn't seem to provide him with a full script. So, he did some research and uncovered the soft-core porn truth about the production company. Feeling very uncomfortable, he backed out, citing a "family emergency."

> "Goals on the road to achievement cannot be achieved without discipline and consistency."
> —Denzel Washington

Building your acting business is a process. For every success story like *Born Champion*, there were countless projects that never came to pass. Either the production would lose its funding before we got started, or worse, I'd shoot the role and they'd run out of money and never finish the film. It was hard not to get demoralized along the way. I wanted things to move faster, to happen immediately. I was often impatient, frustrated by so many highs and lows. The constant stress about money

Headshots, Getting in the Union, and Building Your Résumé

was especially difficult. Sometimes I'd have to decide if I should take a low-paying job as an extra, in hopes of getting a voucher, or take a higher-paying job as an office temp so I could afford new headshots. Prioritizing these various, conflicting needs was taxing. It felt like every decision had the potential to skyrocket or sink my acting career. I didn't know it then, but I know it now: I was living the life of an aspiring actor. So, if you find yourself dealing with these same confusing questions, don't fret—it means you're going through the process the majority of us have also gone through.

For me, what made the struggle even harder was the fact that my friends and family back home couldn't understand "what was taking so long." I began to dread any type of conversation with people back in St. Louis. It's not their fault; they just cared about me and wanted the best for me. But they simply couldn't relate to my world. It was impossible to explain that I was actually doing quite well, all things considered. But how to convince them that the small black box play I was doing was actually a great achievement? Or that the commercial callback was a stepping stone, even though I didn't get the job? They couldn't see the value of these small milestones. They just wanted to know when I would be on TV. Because that's what translated as success to them.

Of the group of people I began my Hollywood journey with, I'm the only one who stayed. Most gave up within two years, went back to their hometowns, or changed careers. It was a lonely feeling when I realized I was the only one left. But I wasn't ready to throw in the towel. I got through those years by constantly reminding myself of the advice from Molly Shannon: Never give up. Say it again: Never give up. One more time: Never give up.

> "It does not matter how slowly you go as long as you do not stop."
> —Confucius

After three years of not giving up, of hustling as an extra and submitting myself for any work I could find, I'd actually made some progress. I'd earned my SAG card, joined a theater company, taken additional acting classes, and worked a bunch of non-union gigs. Not giant leaps, but baby steps. Progress. Here's what my résumé looked like after three years:

Jenna Fischer
SAG

FILM

Born Champion	Lead	American Film Partners
The Specials	Supporting	Mindfire/Brillstein-Grey
Lucky 13	Supporting	John Saviano/Prod
Sex: A Comedy*	Supporting	Regis Arts
Channel 493	Lead	Odin Valkar/Dir

Nominated Best Supporting Actress: Northeast Regional Film Festival

THEATER

Nosferatu	Lead	Zoo District, LA
Annie's Play	Lead	Hudson Guild Theatre, LA
Bunny and Clyde	Lead	Upstage Productions
Boys Next Door	Lead	H&A Theatre
Schoolhouse Rock	Lead	Wooten Lab Theatre
Hamlet	Lead	Shakespeare Festival
Noises Off	Supporting	NMSU

TRAINING
B.A. Theatre: Northeast Missouri State University
Commedia Dell'Arte: Jon Kellam
Hudson Guild Theatre Company
Lyric Self/Stanislavski: John Schmor
Method & Comedy: Lee Orchard
Ballet, tap, and jazz 11 yrs./Member of American Dance Troupe: Mark Krupinski
Affiliate of Zoo District Theatre Company

SPECIAL SKILLS
Water Skiing, Animal Handling, Bowling

The difference between this résumé and the one I started with is obvious. As you can see, I was steadily building my business. And now I finally possessed a set of attributes that a theatrical agent could work with. So now it was time to find one.

CHAPTER THREE
HOW TO FIND, GET, AND KEEP AN AGENT OR MANAGER

"When I wasn't working, I put the blame directly where it belonged—I blamed my agent. When I didn't have an agent, I spent time looking for a new agent so I would have somebody to blame."
—GEORGE BURNS

I like to think of my acting career as if it's a corporation, and I am both the product and the CEO. Like many startup businesses, mine began with a big idea and a lot of grit. From my kitchen table I built my business by submitting headshots and résumés, which sometimes led to auditions and even some work. And today, my business is an actual tax-paying corporation with its own federal ID number and everything. Pretty crazy. In the beginning, though, my corporation was more like a nonprofit. There were only so many jobs that I could get on my own, and those jobs usually didn't pay very well. Since the only way to regularly gain access to professional union jobs is through a theatrical agent or manager, I eventually had to acquire one for my company.

Remember, you don't want to find just *any* agent and/or manager. You want good, smart, hard-working people. So, don't start the search until you're ready, or else you'll end up with some dude who works out of his car.

You have the best chance of landing a good agent or manager when at least three of the following four are true:

You are a trained actor.
You have professional headshots.
You are in the union or close to being in the union.
You have some professional credits/experience under your belt.

If you've been following my advice, you should be right on track. If you bought this book and skipped ahead to this chapter (something I probably would have done), stop, go back, and read about how to get yourself ready. As my grandpa always said, "You need to sharpen the axe before you cut down the tree. The job goes faster that way."

THEATRICAL AGENTS AND MANAGERS: THE BASICS

Some actors have an agent, some have a manager, and some have both. I have both. Let's talk about their specific jobs and responsibilities, because they're not interchangeable. Each has a very specific role.

Agents typically represent hundreds of different actors: dramatic, comedic, musical, young, old, new, and seasoned. Their job is to find work for all of these different actors.

Agents at the small- and medium-sized agencies (the ones you should be pursuing) spend most of their time browsing the Breakdowns. The Breakdowns are a compilation of the available acting jobs posted by casting directors each day. The Breakdowns are only available to agents and managers, not regular folks like you and me. They cannot be found on casting websites. Agents look over the Breakdowns, match their clients to the available roles, and submit them for auditions. If an agent has five clients that match the description of a role, they will submit all five clients to the casting director for consideration. So, you can be competing for work even among the other clients at your agency.

Managers, on the other hand, represent a smaller group of actors and are more capable of giving you personalized attention. Managers often specialize in one aspect of the business, such as comedy, drama, or musical talent. And they don't generally pack their client list with a bunch of duplicates. While an agent may represent ten to twelve sexy Hispanic females, a manager only has one or two. You are more likely to stand out to your manager because you are unique on their roster.

> "Shakespeare said, 'Kill all the lawyers.' There were no agents then."
> —Robin Williams

Managers help you develop an overall business plan and a strategy for making it happen. A good manager has relationships with casting directors, producers, directors, writers, network and studio executives, and other industry professionals. Your manager should be able to set general meetings, thereby opening doors for you to meet important people in the industry. They'll talk you up and get people excited about you. In general, agents, especially the ones at the smaller and medium-sized agencies, don't have time to work with you on this kind of a personal level. They're too busy combing through the daily Breakdowns, trying to get everyone some work. A good manager will also have access to the Breakdowns, so they can coordinate with your agent if they see a role that is right for you. Or, if you don't have an agent, they can submit you to the casting director themselves.

Agents are required to be licensed by the state. Managers are not. So, that dude in the car I mentioned earlier? He can print business cards and call himself a manager—so beware! More new actors are scammed by phony managers than by phony agents.

> **SCAM ALERT: Agents and managers should *never* charge you a startup fee or monthly fee as a term of their representation.** *All legitimate agents and managers operate on commission only.* Agents and managers only make money if *you* make money. If you make zero dollars from acting, they make zero dollars from you.

I've had many agents in my career, but I've only had one manager, Naomi Odenkirk. Naomi and I have been working together for over fifteen years. She has been instrumental in shaping my career, guiding me and growing my business. Together, we created a strategy for concentrating my career in the area of television comedy. While my agent was trying to get me auditions, Naomi was setting me up on general meetings with comedy casting directors so they could get to know me. In fact, Naomi set a general meeting with Allison Jones, the casting director of *The Office*, and you know the rest of that story.

When I get overwhelmed or nervous about a particular job or audition, I can call Naomi crying and freaking out, and she'll be there for me. When I wanted to quit acting, I called her and she talked me off the ledge. (Metaphorical ledge, as I was actually just lying in my bed.) When I told her I wanted to produce my own film and write my own book, she said "Let's make it happen!" I can't tell you how good it feels to know that Naomi is in my corner and on my team—that we're in it together. Having that sense of security is invaluable in this business. If you are lucky enough to find a person like this, swoop them up immediately. But first you have to find them.

HOW TO FIND AN AGENT OR MANAGER

Be Seen

Let's look back in time, to 1998. I had been in Los Angeles three years and had finally found my groove. I'd just finished filming *Born Champion*, my first leading role in a non-union feature film. I was now busy rehearsing a one-act play festival for my theater company and taking weekly acting classes. To make ends meet, I was working two day jobs, plus doing some catering on the weekends. Any free time I had was spent at my kitchen table, mailing headshots and résumés to agents, producers, and casting directors (and eating Lucky Charms).

It was around this time that my old hometown friend Sean Gunn asked me if I'd be willing to do a small role in a live pilot performance that his friend was producing at the HBO Workspace, a tiny theater in Hollywood that often showcased new talent. They needed someone who could play a high school student and Sean thought of me. The showcase was written by an up-and-coming comedy actor from Chicago named Jim Zulevic. Jim had written a comedy pilot script as a way of showcasing himself and his friends from the Chicago-based improvisation group, The Second City.

> "Sometimes you can have the smallest role in the smallest production and still have a big impact."
> —Neil Patrick Harris

I read the script and found it really funny but was a little bummed to see that my particular role was very small. It consisted of maybe seven lines, a few in the first scene and a few in the last. Saying yes to the project meant I would spend most of rehearsal sitting around watching other people perform. It wasn't a very showy role, and I didn't see how performing in it could benefit me personally. I was busy! I didn't have time to be doing small roles like this! If it hadn't been for Sean, I probably would have said no. Luckily, I said yes.

As I suspected, I spent most of the time sitting in the audience watching other people act, but they were really funny people doing great material. It was a total blast. This was my first glimpse into the world of the Second City performers. *These people are hilarious*, I thought. *I want to be around more people like this!*

But, as I predicted, we did the showcase and nothing happened for me professionally. No big deal, as it was a fun experience. I learned a lot. I went back to my kitchen table and stack of headshots. Then, about six months later, Jim called and said he was doing it again, and asked if I would please come back to reprise my role. I said yes, eager to again hang around all of those funny people. Again, I had a total blast, but there was no professional movement. At this point I didn't care. I liked these people and it was fun to perform with them. So, back to my kitchen. And then, not long after, Jim called a *third* time. You can probably guess what I said after I said "Hello?" I said, "Of course, Jim! I'm in!" (Is that what you guessed?)

Well, third time's a charm, because after that *third* performance, Jim's manager approached me in the lobby. She said, "Hi, my name is Naomi Odenkirk. I'm Jim's manager. I love what you're doing up there. It's so simple, but funny, and I can't seem to get it out of my mind. I'd love to meet with you and talk about representation. Do you have a manager?" I pretended like I wasn't peeing my pants with excitement (just a few drops). We exchanged information and set a date to meet for coffee. And Naomi has been my manager ever since.

This kind of pivotal experience is exactly what I want for you. It's why I've been hounding you for two chapters to get out there and get in some projects. The very best way to advance your career

How to Find, Get, and Keep an Agent or Manager

From left: Me, my manager Naomi Odenkirk, Derek Waters, and Naomi's then-assistant Mandy Kahn

is to *be seen*. Nobody will see you in your kitchen, except your creepy neighbor! Student films, short films, showcases, improv shows, web series, standup, YouTube videos, play readings, street performing—you never know where they're going to lead. The more work you do, the more people see you, the more likely the right people are to find you.

Paid Showcases

An often-debated method of getting seen by an agent is through participating in paid showcases. Paid showcases are exactly what their name suggests: Independent companies charge you a fee to meet and audition for an agent (or casting director). Some people swear by them; some people get nowhere.

When I first moved to town, I got a job interning for a company that offered paid showcases to new actors. I worked there for free—making coffee, filing, taking out the trash—in exchange for attending their showcases for free. On the evening of a showcase, it was my job to set up the room, manage the actor sign-in sheet, greet the agent upon arrival, and present him or her with the headshots of the actors who would be auditioning that evening. Then, after everything was set up, I was allowed to participate in the showcase and perform for the agent. At the end of the showcase I had to linger with the agent, making sure they weren't bothered by over-eager actors. It was an amazing opportunity. And it eventually paid off: I signed with an agent that I met at the showcase series.

I include this story because it's a great example of how to separate yourself from the pack. Not only had I found a way to do paid showcases *without paying*, which was essential for me, but I'd also created an opportunity for me to get personal time with agents. When you're getting started in this business, it's stuff like this that makes all the difference. There are ways to break out and stand out; you just have to find them. Be savvy and creative. Think outside the box! You'd be surprised how many opportunities for free classes are available if you are willing/able to intern your time.

I would normally advise against paying for access to agents or casting directors, but paid showcases can be fruitful. Not only do they provide an opportunity to meet industry professionals and hear them speak about the business, they also provide an opportunity to practice the audition process. If you have some extra money, it might not be a bad idea to give one a try. But, *be smart and do your research*. Ask around to find out which companies provide the best access. And before signing up, be sure to ask if you'll be performing for an agent or an assistant. If it's for an assistant, skip it. You want to be in front of decision makers. And check the roster of agents promised to be in attendance to make sure the agencies are a match for you. Don't waste your time and money performing for an agent that wouldn't be a good fit in the first place.

> **SCAM ALERT: If you don't live in Los Angeles or New York, do not attend a paid showcase.** There is no way that attending a paid showcase in Iowa or Nebraska or Dallas is going to end with you getting a Hollywood agent. Trust me, legitimate Hollywood talent agents are not flying into the heartland and scouring the cities for new talent. I *begged* my parents to sign up for one of these when I was a teenager in St. Louis. Thankfully, they were smart enough to know that it wasn't a legitimate showcase, it was simply a way to take advantage of young people's big dreams and sell them acting classes and headshots.

Get Personal Recommendations

Referrals are a very effective method of meeting people in this business. If you've developed a good relationship with a casting director, director, or producer, consider asking if they'd recommend you to an agent. But don't be annoying about it. You don't want to ruin a budding professional relationship by pestering people for help advancing your career. What do I mean by annoying? If you book a role with a casting director for the first time, and then immediately ask them for a favor, you're being annoying. But if you've been called in to a casting office consistently and done well over a long period of time, chances are you won't annoy them if you ask for a recommendation. Unless you ask at an annoying time, or in an annoying way, or in an annoying voice. If this sounds like you, pick up my next book, *How to Stop Being Annoying!*

Don't be afraid to let anyone and everyone know about your search for an agent. Your recommendation may come from a very unlikely place. My friend got a meeting with an agent when she told someone at her high school reunion about her search. Little did she know, her old high school friend had a cousin working as an agent in Hollywood. She put in a good word and got her friend a meeting.

Send Blind Submissions and Cover Letters

If you aren't able to get a personal recommendation for a meeting, and if you aren't successful in a showcase, your next best option for meeting an agent is through blind submissions. Send a headshot, résumé, and cover letter introducing yourself to an agent (or manager) and hope the agent calls you in for a meeting. It's rare to get representation via a blind submission, but it happens. When you're an aspiring actor, you have to try anything and everything.

However, "blind submission" doesn't mean thoughtless submission. Be smart. Do your homework. Research the various agencies, their number of clients, their specialties, their number of years in the business. Do you want to specialize in television? Find an agency that does too. If you don't have a lot of credits, look for agents that specialize in taking on newcomers. Be realistic. If you are new in town, don't bother submitting to Creative Artists Agency (CAA).

You can find more information about talent and management agencies online, by going to *Backstage*'s Call Sheet. It lists all of the agencies, their specialties, and even tells you their preferred method for blind submissions. You'll want to submit to a specific agent, not the agency as a whole.

Write a good cover letter. Sorry, but I honestly can't think of a task more boring than writing a cover letter. Maybe researching talent agencies online? Oh, but you've done that already! So now it's time for the letters. Keep them short and sweet. Don't repeat the information on your résumé; tell them something new. To help you get started, I asked an agent friend to give me an example of a cover letter that caught his eye. His agency is known for representing standup comedians and sketch comedy performers. He liked this letter because it was specific and pointed out the ways that this person was a self-starter. (*Note: I've taken the liberty of changing a few identifying details of the letter.*)

> *Hello, my name is Martin Chen, and I am a working actor/writer specializing in comedy.*
>
> *I am a sketch performer at UCB and iO West and was a cast member of the 2012 CBS Diversity Showcase. Last year, I performed in a sketch comedy show with my brother, which I wrote. As a comedy duo, we recently started releasing online sketch comedy in Korean (with English subtitles). Attached is a link to one of our latest episodes.*
>
> *I am an extremely versatile actor and writer who would very much like to meet with you to discuss representation. I am trying to find someone who will hopefully be able to give me more opportunities to help me take my career to the next level.*
>
> *I have attached a copy of my résumé and headshot and here is a link to my reel. My recent guest appearance on* Key & Peele *airs this week. It was a fantastic experience to work with them.*
>
> *Best,*
>
> *Martin*

I like this letter, too. It's short and informative. Timing his letter just before the airing of a guest appearance was a great move. Martin clearly researched this agency and knew they specialized in comedy. If his supporting materials were good, I'd call him in if I were an agent. He seems focused, realistic, and professional.

After you've sent out your letter, it's a good idea to follow up with a postcard or email, if you haven't heard back. But be cautious. It is possible to be too aggressive. The best time to follow up is when you have some new information to share: a new guest appearance, a new relationship with a casting director, a play, a new reel, a new headshot. Just don't overdo it. Too many pokes can be annoying, and that's not the kind of attention you want.

Be Seen 2: How to Make Your Own Luck

A successful career in the entertainment business could not be achieved without a little bit of luck. Establishing good luck isn't just about being in the right place at the right time. It's about making the kinds of choices that put you in the right place at the right time. If your goal is to find an agent, you're much more likely to be in the right place at the right time if you're busy doing showcases, plays, and taking classes. Chances are you won't be in the right place at the right time if you're spending your days eating Lucky Charms on your couch. Trust me, I tried.

I've told you how I met my first agent. But I haven't told you how I met my first *great* agent. After about 300 bowls of Lucky Charms, I finally left my apartment and went to see a friend's improv show. It was there that I met a theater director named Jon Kellam, who persuaded me to sign up for his Commedia del Arte class. It seemed a little artsy-fartsy to me, so I hesitated and made some excuses about money. But when he told me the class was free, I didn't have any good reason to say no. Well, thank goodness I said yes! Because it was the first step on the road to meeting my first *great* agent!

> "Luck is what happens when preparation meets opportunity."
> —Seneca

In case you are not familiar with Commedia, it is a highly stylized form of acting in which you choose one of four emotions—fear, joy, sadness, or anger—and perform them in an exaggerated way and switch between emotions from line to line. I looked forward to

Actor Joe Fria and me during a performance of Nosferatu, *1999*

the class each week. It was nothing like the style of acting I'd been studying.

While in class, Jon started to develop his idea for a musical version of the film *Nosferatu* to be done in the Commedia style. To his credit, this was an insane idea—totally nuts and totally fun. Jon eventually took the project to the Zoo District theater company, and I was cast as the young lover Mina. We put up the play in an abandoned warehouse in the middle of downtown Los Angeles.

Performing in *Nosferatu* was not something I did to get noticed. I did it because it was challenging, I liked the people involved, and I needed an outlet for my creativity. To this day, it continues to be one of the most exciting things I've ever done. The role required me to dye my hair black and perform in full Kabuki makeup. It was a high-energy show, totally exhilarating.

But this wasn't really the type of project that attracted industry professionals. For one, the theater was in a very rundown and dangerous part of town. Every night I went to the theater, I got a little frightened after I parked my car. It was desolate and dark and had weird people hanging out on the street corners. So, for a person to pay money for this show, they had to *really, really* love experimental theater.

Luckily, the Zoo District has a loyal group of sponsors who love just that. This was my audience. So, imagine my surprise when, one night after the show, the box office manager handed me an envelope. Inside was a business card from an agent, let's call him Charlie, along with a note asking if we could meet regarding representation.

Even though I had an agent, the one from the paid showcase, I wasn't totally happy with her. I told Naomi about Charlie's request for a meeting. Her advice was that we should talk with the people at my current agency first and let them know I was unsatisfied. We did. Nothing changed. So I left the agency.

We went in to meet Charlie. He said he loved my performance, thought I had real talent, and, despite my dismal résumé, would like to sign me as a client. I couldn't believe my luck! He was a legit agent at a well-respected, medium-sized, SAG-accredited agency. I signed with him. He introduced me to the other agents in his office, and we were off and running. I was so relieved and excited. I finally had an awesome agent who believed in me!

So, all it took for me to get my first great agent was to live in Los Angeles for three years, take a wacky acting class, and perform a stylized Commedia musical based on a classic horror film in Kabuki makeup at a scary theater in a dangerous section of downtown Los Angeles! Easy breezy!

In all honesty, I got lucky. But it wasn't just blind luck, it was the kind of luck I wrote about earlier. I was living an active artistic life, performing in a play, surrounded by other like-minded artists. I wasn't waiting for things to happen to me; I was out there making them happen. So, when Charlie walked into the theater that night and saw me perform, it was the culmination of events that I had set in motion months in advance. Imagine if Charlie had met me in a coffee shop. Would I really have ended up his client? Doubtful. He signed me because he saw me act and was taken with my talent, Kabuki makeup and all.

MEETING WITH AN AGENT (OR MANAGER OR CASTING DIRECTOR)

Okay, an agent got your submission, or saw you perform, and wants to meet. Yay! Put on your dancing shoes! Actually, don't do that. Just put on regular shoes and be yourself. The meeting will be a chance for the agent to get to know your personality and get a sense of what type of roles you might naturally be right for. They've most likely seen your reel and they've read about your credits. So, when the agent says, "Hello, tell me a little about yourself," unless you just booked a role in the next Quentin Tarantino film through a submission in *Backstage*, don't start the meeting by prattling on and on about your acting career. Talk about your *life* outside of the business. Look for common ground. Be a cool person to talk with. The agent wants to get to know *you* and decide if you're a person they'll enjoy working with for the next, hopefully, several years. If you're annoying or difficult, they may pass on you, so no dancing shoes. Oh, and no Starbucks. Leave your coffee in the car.

After the small talk is over, the agent might ask you questions like, "What are your goals? What are you hoping to do? What type of acting interests you?" This is your cue to start talking business. When initially asked questions like this, I would always make the mistake of saying "Oh my gosh, everything! I'd love to do television or film, drama or comedy, studio films or independent films, theater . . . I do it all! I'm not picky!" This seemed like the right answer. I wanted to show I was easy to work with and open to anything. But upon hearing this response, my manager, Naomi, set me straight. She said that answer is way too general and needs to be more specific.

So, that's when I started answering the question like this: "I love doing comedy. I'm mainly interested in booking roles in television comedy because, eventually, I'd love to be on an ensemble comedy with a lot of characters like *Cheers*, which, incidentally, is what inspired me to pursue acting." And sometimes I would add, "I also love doing dramatic roles that have a comedic element like something you might see in a Coen Brothers film. If there's a drama needing a little comedy relief, I'd love to do that."

> "A lot of people are afraid to say what they want. That's why they don't get what they want."
> —Madonna

I'm a big believer in specificity when it comes to manifesting successes in your life. The more specific you can be about your goals, the more likely you are to achieve them, and the more an agent can help you achieve them. As CEO of your acting company, part of your job is to inspire your representatives to action with your specificity and enthusiasm.

Agent Auditions

Quite often agents ask prospective clients to perform a scene or monologue in their initial meeting. Be prepared for this request, so you're not frantically memorizing the night before. Always have a comedic scene, dramatic scene, comedic monologue, and dramatic monologue at your fingertips. If you are a stage actor, you should have eighteen bars of a song and a Shakespearean monologue too. Even if you have an amazing reel and credits, the agent may still ask you to read. It's important for them to see how you do *live* in a room, under pressure, because this is how casting directors will be seeing you.

As for which scene or monologue you choose, aim for material that is around three to five minutes in length, and think practically. Chances are you'll be performing in a tiny office or conference room, so don't pick something that involves a lot of yelling or big movements or complicated blocking. Don't wear a costume, unless you want to seem like a complete loon. And don't do material that will make people uncomfortable. No guns, no violence, no smoking, no nudity. While you might be an amazing dramatic actor, no one wants to sit through a five-minute graphic rape monologue on a Tuesday morning.

Most importantly, *pick material that is appropriate to how you would most likely be cast*. This is a chance for you to show the agent that you understand how you will be marketed. You will have plenty of chances to show your range down the line. Remember that most film and television roles are pretty vanilla. The agents just need to see that you can act. Aim to do a solid job. I used to perform a comedic monologue I found in a book of monologues—you can find these at most drama bookstores or libraries—about a shy girl who belly flops off the high dive in high school. It was simple, funny, and charming with a suspenseful story. It killed.

You may also be asked to perform a "cold read." This means you will be presented with a scene upon arrival, given about fifteen to twenty minutes in the waiting room to prepare, and then asked to perform. Agents need to know you can perform on your feet, as it's common to be handed new materials at a casting session or even after you've gotten the job on set. If you're not confident in your cold reading ability, there are classes that concentrate on mastering the skill. Consider taking one. You can be the greatest actor in the world, but if you can't do an effective cold read, you'll be stuck acting in your living room.

PICKING YOUR REPRESENTATION

Remember, this is a *mutual* interview. You need to determine if this is a person you'd trust with your career. So, don't be blinded by the size or name of the agency. The most important thing is the individual agent, because ultimately that's who you're agreeing to team up with.

Is this a person who will take your calls? Someone who will be passionate and engaged in getting you to the next level? Do you like this person? And most importantly: Do they believe in you?

I've had several agents over my many years. I had agents that truly believed in me and others that just took me on because they liked my photo and credits. I found that the agents that truly believed in me worked harder than the ones for whom I was just a good business decision.

My first agent—the one I met at the paid showcase—never seemed very passionate about me. We never talked or strategized about my career. In the two years that I was her client, she only got me a handful of auditions.

When I signed with Charlie everything was different. He wasn't just playing a numbers game; he was truly enthusiastic about me as an artist. When we first started working together, he took the time to ask me what type of work I wanted to do, then set about helping me realize my vision. Along with Naomi, we created a strategy for growing my career. Charlie started small, sending me out for roles with just one or two lines. Then after I'd landed a couple of these, he began sending me out for guest-starring roles. Then eventually series regular roles. He took the time to slowly build my résumé with desirable credits and coached me on what to expect at different auditions. I still remember when he spent forty-five minutes late one evening, talking me through the long process of auditioning to be a series regular on a television show. I was so grateful and much less nervous at my network audition the next day. Charlie's dedication was genuine. He would follow up with casting directors after my auditions, getting notes on my performance, which was so important in helping me improve and refine my audition skills. It's this type of relationship that you want with your representatives. You might hear the phrase, "Any agent is better than no agent." I disagree. The worst thing you can have is an agent who doesn't work for you. Because it will keep you from meeting the agent that will.

How to Find, Get, and Keep an Agent or Manager

Agent/Manager Contracts: Standards and Scams

Legitimate agents only take 10 percent of your earnings from acting. Managers also take 10 percent of your earnings from acting. So, if you have both a manager and an agent, you have to give 10 percent to your agent *plus* 10 percent to your manager. That means, right off the top, you are giving away 20 percent of your income to your representatives. (You didn't know I was also a math genius, did you?) But remember, you are running a business. No company keeps 100 percent of its profits. Provided your representatives are helping to grow your business, they are worth the investment.

When it's time to take the plunge, your agent may ask you to sign a contract. This is normal. However, you want to be smart before you sign anything. A standard agency contract is one year to start, followed by three years at re-signing.

You can find an example of a standard agency contract on the SAG-AFTRA website. They also provide a list of SAG-AFTRA–certified agents. Check to see if the agent you are considering is on the list. If you fear you have been scammed, let the union know. SAG-AFTRA has some control over agents and, if you are a union member, can protect you from a bad agency contract. However, SAG-AFTRA *cannot* protect you from a bad manager. So, again, be sure to *read the whole contract* before you sign anything.

MAINTAINING THE AGENT/ CLIENT RELATIONSHIP

Once you have signed with an agent, it's important to develop a relationship with them. You are not their only client, so you want to be on their mind as they're browsing the Breakdowns each day. Of course, the best way to stand out is to book jobs. But in the meantime, try and get to know your agent as a person. What do they like? Do they have kids? Pets? Like to cook? Favorite sports team? As a mother, I can tell you the fastest way to my heart is to take an interest in my kids. For example, my son is currently in love with the solar system. If I were an agent and you were my client, it would be a great idea to send me a link to the latest photos from the New Horizons spacecraft with a little note that said, "I saw these today and thought Weston might love them."

Sometimes developing a rapport requires work, and sometimes it just comes naturally. With Charlie, it came naturally. I loved chatting with Charlie. He especially loved two things: Fonzie and *Survivor*. One Christmas I gave him a Fonzie doll, which was a big hit. Another time, I stopped by with a signed photo of our favorite *Survivor* castmate (Charlie and I were always discussing the latest episode of *Survivor*). Our relationship had a genuine give and take, and both of these gestures were authentic. People can feel when you have a real interest or a calculated one.

It can be as simple as dropping by once a month with their favorite coffee from Starbucks. The trick is to go in without any expectations. Just drop off the coffee and say hello, and be on your way. That's really all you need. Be noticed without being annoying.

On a purely professional level, you definitely want to consult your agent when deciding on new headshots or making a new acting reel. These are the tools they'll be using to sell you, so you want them to fall in love with your materials. You should also make them aware of new relationships you're developing with industry professionals. If you participated in a showcase with a certain casting director, let your agent know. It's good ammunition for the next time they submit you to that casting office.

I know some actors who are constantly pestering their agents about various auditions, saying stuff like, "My friend went in for a guest spot on *Walking Dead*. Why didn't you get me an audition for that? I'd be perfect!" I can't recommend you do this, although I have been guilty of doing it myself a time or two. There's nothing worse than feeling overlooked or forgotten, right? But ultimately, you have to manage your insecurities and trust that your agent is submitting you for every role for which you're qualified.

> "The reason actors, artists, and writers have agents is because we'll do it for nothing."
> —Morgan Freeman

You can also help your agent by continuing to find work for yourself. Keep doing plays, short films, and student films. Continue to add new and better material to your reel. Don't stop hustling just because you have an agent.

However, don't overstep your bounds. You'll most likely regret it, like I once did. Back when I was starting out, I had heard about actors getting jobs by crashing auditions and blowing away the casting directors. So, I decided to try it. I had a friend who had a friend who worked for an agent and had access to the Breakdowns. We each paid her $25 a week to secretly email them to us. Shady, right? Even though I had an agent, I wanted to see all the roles that were available. And then one time I took the shadiness a step further. I saw a listing for a TV drama that was perfect for me, and my agent didn't get me an audition. So, I consulted the Breakdown, got the information for the casting office, and set out to get the role myself.

My big plan was to go into the casting office with the excuse of dropping off a new headshot. This wasn't an entirely unheard of thing to do, especially if you had a relationship with the casting office already. It was normal to pop in, greet the receptionist, and say, "Hi!

Just wanted to drop off this new headshot so you had my latest one on file. Thanks! Have a nice day!"

Well, the problem was I'd never been to this casting office before, so doing a random drop-off was risky. My plan was sent awry the moment I arrived. Before I could even speak, the woman at the front desk said, "Are you here for the audition? The sign-in sheet is over there." Wow, that was easy. So instead of correcting her, I just signed in and sat down with a copy of the scene. I was feeling good. I had this. After all, I was perfect for the role, right?

A few minutes later, the casting director came out and started scanning the sign-in list. Suddenly I hear my name, very loud. "Jenna Fischer?" I stood up and walked toward her with my hand outstretched. But instead of shaking my hand, she crossed her arms and sternly said, "I didn't call you in. Who are you?" Uh oh. I started a verbal tap dance: "Oh, I'm sorry. I think I'm as confused as you are. I came in to drop off my new headshot and the woman at the front said to go ahead and sign in, so I thought maybe she wanted me to read, and . . ." She cut me off: "Stop it. No, you didn't. That's not what happened, and you weren't confused. I know what you're trying to do; you're trying to crash this audition, aren't you? Get out." Oof. Caught red-handed. I picked up my stuff and left, totally humiliated.

But the embarrassment didn't end there. She called my agent and told him to never submit me, that she would never want to see me again. This really stung. I'd just completely burned a bridge to one of the top five casting directors for television dramas. And I needed bridges! I was treading water all over town! Luckily, Charlie didn't drop me as a client. He yelled at me pretty good, though. My only recourse was to admit that I had messed up and to promise to never do it again. And true to her word, the casting director never called me in again.

In this particular instance, my risk-taking didn't pay off with a job. It was a bummer to feel so humiliated and completely destroy a potential relationship. But while she never saw me after that, she never saw me *before* that either, so I justified it by saying I hadn't lost anything anyway. The upside of this whole crazy saga was that I had gotten my agent's attention. He certainly couldn't blame me for not having gumption. As strange as that sounds, sometimes you have to be the crazy one to get noticed. Well, he noticed me, all right.

Listen, it's normal to get frustrated when you feel like things aren't moving as quickly as you would like. Don't be afraid to talk with your agent if you aren't getting any auditions. That's their job. If your agent claims to be sending you out and yet he's not securing you any auditions, ask him what he thinks the problem may be. Has he followed up with casting directors for feedback? The way he responds will tell you a lot about how he perceives you. Can he provide you with constructive feedback and respectfully suggest ways to change the situation? Or, does he hedge, defend, and abuse?

The best way to find and keep a great agent is to be a great client. Take initiative; stay up to date with your headshot, résumé, and reel; be realistic

> "Only I can change my life, no one can do it for me."
> —Carol Burnett

and professional; and never stop working hard to create opportunities for yourself. There's a reason that an agent only gets 10 percent of your payment: It's because they only do 10 percent of the work. You have to do the other 90 percent. Remember, you are the CEO and the product. Nobody is ever going to care for your career as much as you do, so keep the company and the product in tip-top shape. Find a great agent or manager, but don't expect them to do all the work. Keep yourself active, and you will keep yourself moving forward.

CHAPTER FOUR
AUDITIONING, REJECTION, AND HOW TO PERSEVERE

"I don't think actors should ever expect to get a role, because the disappointment is too great. You've got to think of things as an opportunity. An audition's an opportunity to have an audience."
—AL PACINO

Audition. The dreaded audition. Every actor has horror stories about auditioning. I am certainly no exception. Take, for example, the time I auditioned for Larry David, legendary creator of *Seinfeld* and *Curb Your Enthusiasm*. I went in for a small role on *Curb* and I got a call from my agent saying the casting director wanted me to come back and read again. But get this: I was going to be reading *with Larry personally*. Not only would I be meeting one of my idols, I'd be performing with him. Keep in mind, *Curb Your Enthusiasm* is an improvised show, so there's no script to work from. Basically, they give the actors a general outline for the scene and then the actors improvise, making up the dialogue in the moment. I had taken improv classes and even done improv auditions before, but never with a scene partner like Larry David! My stomach was in knots. I'm pretty sure my voice was shaking. In the scene, I was supposed to pretend to see him in a store, corner him, and ask if he was coming to my son's birthday party, since I had never received his RSVP. Simple enough, right? They said "action" and I performed the scene, walking up and delivering the exact line they had pitched me moments before. And then . . . my mind went blank. I just stood there, frozen, looking at Larry, offering nothing else. I just kept muttering, "You didn't RSVP." It was so incredibly awkward, a total bomb. The audition petered out, and I headed for the door. As I was walking out, Larry stood to say, "Thanks for coming in." I misinterpreted his gesture, for some reason thinking he wanted to hug me goodbye. I thought it was unusual to hug goodbye at the end of an audition, but since I'd already tanked the audition, I didn't want to be rude as well. As he moved toward me, I opened my arms and moved toward him, prepared to meet him halfway. Inches from hugging him, I realized he was just gesturing to the door, not opening his arms for a hug. Ugh. It was too late. I was already hugging Larry David.

There was also the time that I auditioned for the lead in a new television show. I was so nervous that I broke down crying after I messed up a line. Messing up a line is not a big deal, but for some reason, on that day, it broke me. It was an over-the-top reaction, totally out of place for such a small mistake. I went from seeming totally normal to ugly-crying in a matter of seconds. Through the sobs, I begged them to let me start over. They were nice and let me begin again, but it didn't matter, I could barely get through the scene as I was still choking back tears. How embarrassing! At the time, this felt like a catastrophic mistake. In my mind, I had totally ruined my reputation all over town. Little did I know that bad auditions are a part of the process. If you totally bomb at an audition, try to be kind to yourself. It's normal. Just another part of the life of an actor.

For as long as I can remember, I've always had to battle nervousness, in auditions and in life. I'm sure most actors do. We are naturally sensitive people. In the past, I've found myself so nervous at auditions that I can feel my teeth throbbing in my mouth as I try to talk. I have a friend who gets so nervous she farts in the waiting room, and sometimes even in the audition room. So, if you feel like a neurotic mess every time you have an audition, don't fret; at least you're not stinking up the place (*badum-ching!*).

When I was a struggling actor, the most unnerving part of an audition was having to sit in the waiting room, surrounded by other actresses who looked exactly like me. I remember the pit I felt in my stomach when, fresh off the highway from Missouri, I entered my first Los Angeles casting agency and found myself staring at a room full of curly-haired, Midwestern twenty-somethings. It was a sobering moment. I soon realized that this was the norm; the competition was fierce and I would see versions of myself at every audition in Los Angeles. After this initial eye-opening experience, whenever I entered an audition waiting room, I would secretly size up the competition while I walked toward the sign-in sheet. Then I'd scan the list of names and note all of the various agencies that represented them. My brain did all kinds of mental gymnastics. *She has a bigger agent than me . . . I've never heard of her agent . . . blah, blah, blah.* Then, when I took my seat, I'd flip-flop between all the reasons I was getting the part, and all the reasons I wasn't. Of course, this was all in my head. To the outside observer, I appeared calm and confident, just sitting and looking at my audition materials, making little notes with a pen, pretending that I was totally at ease.

I was really bothered by the nerves. I tried all kinds of methods to calm them down. I swore off caffeine before auditions, tried listening to soothing music on the car ride over, took deep breaths in the bathroom before going into the room. I even tried chatting nicely with the other actors in the waiting room. When that didn't work, I tried *not* chatting with the other actors in the waiting room. None of these methods made a bit of difference. As soon as my name was called, I still had the same throbbing teeth and panicked mind.

However, eventually I found the one ingredient that was helpful in making me less nervous: experience. The more auditions I went on, the more I learned about the process of auditioning, the better I got.

> "I think the most important thing is you have to learn to love auditioning, which I have definitely learned to love. It's going to be a huge part of your career, even if you're right at the top."
> —Megan Park

And the better I got, the less nervous I would become. It wasn't that the nerves disappeared completely. They were still there, bubbling under the surface, but now they had less power over me.

So, don't get down on yourself if it feels clunky for you at first. It took me a long time to figure out the audition process. In my early years, auditions were few and far between. (That's also normal.) With so much down time between auditions, it was hard to build up any momentum. This is why getting yourself into a weekly acting class can be so helpful. It's a great way to keep your instrument in tune. The more you work, the better your work becomes. Even if that "work" is class work.

AUDITIONS STEP BY STEP

Pre-Reads

With most film and television roles, the first step in the audition process is a reading with the casting director. This is commonly called a "pre-read." The pre-read is an opportunity for the casting director to audition a large group of actors and weed out the ones who don't fit the director's vision. The casting director is usually looking for five to ten great people that they can present to the director at the callback. The most important thing to know about a pre-read is that, in most cases, the casting director does not decide who gets the part. More often than not, it is the director or producer who eventually decides. Don't get me wrong: Casting directors have a lot of influence. They will often present their preferences or single out a person they feel is best. But most of the time, the casting director is just one of many people you'll need to impress to get the role. So, at the first set of auditions, you are actually just competing for a callback. But there is more than one callback slot. So, you have better odds than you think!

When you audition for film and television roles, you are frequently given an audition scene to prepare at home. These are commonly referred to as "sides." Sometimes you get the sides a few days before the audition; other times you get them the night before. Don't fret—you are not expected to have the entire scene memorized when you audition. That being said, you should be very familiar with the material.

While it's perfectly acceptable to hold your sides while you audition, keep in mind that the casting director needs to see your face while you're acting. You don't want to be looking down at the sides; you want your face up and out, especially when you first begin. I recommend memorizing at least the first three lines of your script and identifying your character's important emotional moments in the scene. Should you need a line, glance down at the sides and get it. You want to perform the lines as written. Do not paraphrase or improvise unless you're directed to do so.

Most auditions just start with the audition. There isn't a lot of small talk. Don't let this throw you. Sometimes a casting director might help break the ice with a little chitchat, but if it isn't initiated by the casting director or others in the room, don't start it yourself. Also, definitely do not start your audition by making excuses like "I just got these sides an hour ago" or "I just flew in from Japan." But, if you have a question about the character, script, or story, by all means, ask your

Auditioning, Rejection, and How to Persevere 107

question. When I first started out, I was afraid to ask questions. I was worried it would make me look like I didn't know what I was doing. But the truth is that questions that help inform your performance are not only acceptable, they are necessary. My success at auditions improved when I got over my fear of asking questions.

When you audition, you will usually perform the scene with a casting assistant, otherwise known as a "reader," while the casting director watches. There is no rehearsal with the reader. In fact, you will meet the reader mere moments before you perform the scene. Readers are not actors, so you should be prepared for anything. Some readers are good; some are awful. I've had readers that sounded bored, messed up the lines, or skipped ahead accidentally. Sometimes, they perform the scene completely different from how I imagined it would be done. I remember once I had an audition for a five-line role on a cop show. My character was a witness to an armed robbery and was being questioned by a detective. The scene seemed like a pretty straightforward interrogation scene. But the reader was giving it all kinds of flirty undertones. I thought, *Should I continue how I planned? Or should I change my performance to match what the reader is doing?* I decided to just kept going as I'd rehearsed it at home. Then, after I finished, I asked the casting director for some clarification. She gave me some thoughts, and I read again. There have been times I've asked to read again, feeling like I hadn't nailed every beat of the scene, and been told, "No need. We've seen what we needed to see." I've always taken this response to mean I'm not right for the role, or I've failed to impress the casting director. But, according to casting director Allison Jones, most of the time one

> "I knew that I had some sort of baseline of talent, ability, and chutzpah and confidence, but then knowing how to get anyone to pay attention is the big mystery. So I just kept auditioning. I kept showing up and I kept trying. And I kept trying to push down the voice that was saying, 'You're terrible. Someone's better than you. They're going to give the part to the other guy.' And elevate the part of me that said, like, 'You're worth it. You should be here.'"
>
> —Jon Hamm

read is enough, and not being asked to read a second time is not an indication of how you've done.

Most auditions end with a simple "Thanks for coming in." The casting director will not give you feedback in the room. Don't take that to mean you didn't do a good job. It's totally normal. No need to ask, "When are callbacks?" or "When would this shoot?" Let your agent or manager get that information for you.

Callbacks

If the casting director decides you are well suited for the role, you'll get a "callback." This means you will be invited to return to the casting office and audition for a second time. A callback almost always involves reading the same scene as your first audition; however, you may be asked to make some small changes to your performance. If you're not directed to make a change, it means you're doing it right already, so perform exactly as you had in your first audition. Remember, the first audition was only for the casting director, and now you're reading for the director and producers. Even if the casting director put your first reading on tape, assume they are seeing you for the first time and do what you did before. It worked the first time, right? This also pertains to your appearance. Do your hair the same and wear the same outfit. There was a period of time when I wore the exact same red blouse with tiny white polka dots to every single audition. It was the perfect mixture of sweet and a little sexy. Eventually I wore it to a premiere. See ya later, overalls!

Creating a Consistent Body of Work

You cannot possibly get every role you audition for, so don't put that kind of pressure on yourself. It might help to view the audition process

Auditioning, Rejection, and How to Persevere

Me in my red audition blouse at the premiere of American Dreamz, *2006*

as a spiritual journey, focused more on the work rather than the results. Your job is to go in, time and time again, and produce a consistent body of quality acting. Never mind about getting the part; focus on the quality of your auditions. I want to say this again because it's perhaps the most important piece of information in this entire book: *Your job as an actor is to create a consistent body of work.* It is not to book jobs. It is not to worry and beat yourself up over every job you didn't book. Those decisions are out of your control. What is *in* your control is your approach to auditioning. So just because you didn't book a certain role, it doesn't mean you've failed. More often than not, getting or not getting a role has very little to do with how well you performed at that particular audition. It boils down to how you fit into a bigger picture they are painting. If you're consistently having good auditions, you'll be laying the groundwork for future successes. An acting coach once told me that my goal should be to collect fifty "no's" for every one "yes." This actually turned out to be really effective advice. Every time I failed to get a part I'd think, *Cool, I'm one step closer to collecting my fifty no's! Which means I'm one step closer to a yes!*

> "Fail often so you can succeed sooner."
> —Tom Kelley

That same acting coach always preached that actors should forget about booking jobs; just aim for getting callbacks. Because getting a callback means you're making an impression. It means the casting director knows you won't embarrass them when they call you in to read in front of a director. It also means you are building an important relationship. If you are getting lots of callbacks, you will eventually book a job.

Take, for example, the story of how I landed on *The Office*. *The Office* was cast by Allison Jones, who is one of the top casting directors in Los Angeles. She is known for discovering some of the most unusual comedy talents working today. She cast *Freaks and Geeks*, *Curb Your Enthusiasm*, *The 40-Year-Old Virgin*, and *The Office*. She discovered such people as Seth Rogen, James Franco, Jason Segel, Rainn Wilson, Jonah Hill, Aubrey Plaza, Nick Offerman, Adam Scott, and me!

My first audition for Allison was not for *The Office*. It was for a two-line role on the television show *Freaks and Geeks*. I got a callback but didn't get the job. My next audition with Allison was for a series regular role on a new Judd Apatow show called *Undeclared*. I didn't get that either. Later, I auditioned for a one-line role on *Undeclared* and got it! Yay! Finally!

I kept going into her office year after year, auditioning for different parts—small roles, big roles, pilots. (Allison even witnessed the awkward hug with Larry David. Thankfully, she didn't stop calling me in after that embarrassing debacle.) It seemed like every couple of months

Auditioning, Rejection, and How to Persevere

I got a call from Allison to audition. This was a good sign. When the same casting director keeps calling, you know you're doing something right! Even though most of the time I didn't get the part, she kept bringing me back. Over time I developed a relationship with her, not because I schmoozed her at a party or sent her chocolates on her birthday, but by proving that I was a reliable and serious actor capable of providing a *consistent body of work*. If I haven't made it clear yet, having that consistent body of work is truly what this business is all about.

Eventually my consistent body of work with Allison paid off—five years after our first meeting. She remembered me when it was time to cast *The Office*, and my career was changed forever. It didn't matter that I hadn't been cast in all the previous roles for which I'd auditioned. Because in the end, I got the best role of all: I got Pam Beesly.

One of my proudest audition moments was for a really slutty bar maid on a new TV show. The breakdown described the role as a "Pam Anderson type." I called my agent and said, "There must be some mistake. I can never pull this off. I just don't have the sex appeal. I feel stupid. No one is going to take me seriously." He said, "This is what they called you in for. You should go. You never know. Maybe they're going another way with it."

> "If you get a chance to act in a room that somebody else has paid rent for, then you're given a free chance to practice your craft."
> —Philip Seymour Hoffman

"Going another way with it" actually happens a lot. A role that was originally meant for a man goes to a woman. Or the age changes. Or the race. So, I took my agent's advice and gave the best audition I could. Turns out my instincts were correct; I didn't get the job. In fact, I didn't even get a callback. But it was still a positive experience. I had conquered my rambling, fear-driven brain and committed to the audition anyway. And, besides all that, I gave a great audition. I could feel it. I just didn't look like Pam Anderson. (I guess they weren't "going another way" after all.) It was a huge milestone for me. But difficult to explain to relatives at Christmas.

A year later, I got an audition for the role of a trashy prostitute in an independent film called *Employee of the Month*. After my earlier breakthrough, I felt confident this time around. I knew I could pull off this role, even though I wasn't necessarily the type they were looking for. Well, as it turns out, this time they *did* "go another way with it." They thought my performance was funny, an innocent-looking prostitute who talks like a seasoned pro. It was my first significant part in a movie, and I got to shoot two scenes opposite Matt Dillon! Tell that to the folks back home!

Every audition is a chance to learn, practice, and grow as an actor. The success is not always in getting the part but in the seed that is planted. So, don't beat yourself up if you don't get all the parts. Just make sure you are learning, growing, and doing your very best. That's all you can really control. And, listen, casting directors make mistakes all the time. They're only human. Allison Jones once confessed that she failed to bring Ryan Gosling in for a callback.

Self-Taping

An increasingly popular method of auditioning is self-taping. Rather than calling you into a casting office to audition in the room, the casting director asks you to submit a tape of yourself reading the scene. Well, you can imagine the varied quality of the tapes that are submitted. I'm not talking about audition quality; I'm talking about production. There are a number of important production details to consider when self-taping. The most obvious are the picture and sound. Of course, casting directors aren't expecting pristinely produced self-submissions, but the less distraction in your audition tape, the better. Take some time and consider the quality of your self-taping apparatus. Is there decent lighting? How's the sound? Are there any distractions behind you? You'd be surprised how a few small tweaks can drastically increase the quality of your tape (and, thus, your audition). My friend Lindsey bought some lights off Amazon and set up an area solely dedicated to self-taping in her house. This way, when the moment arises, she's ready. She just calls one of her trusted actor friends and starts working on the scene. She's booked roles in two films through self-tape submissions.

If you're unable to create your own self-taping studio, you might ask your agent or manager if they have a resource for self-taping. My manager has a setup at her office that I've used a number of times. Her assistant reads with me, we choose our favorite take, and then upload the video. Simple. If that's not an option, there are places that will help you by putting you on tape for a small fee. But if you have several auditions a month, this can add up. Either way, figure out your strategy for self-taping *now*. The turnaround time is often short between request and submission. You don't want to be scrambling to figure out how to tape yourself when the moment arises. You'll want that time to focus on preparing your audition.

The Value of Studying Audition Technique

Coming out of school, I knew I was a good actor. But how could I *show* people I was a good actor? Sure, I could blow your mind after five weeks of rehearsing the role of Ophelia from *Hamlet*. But how do I stand out when the part only has three lines? How do I prepare to read for a lead role in a pilot when I just received the materials the night before? Or, even worse, ten minutes before being called into the room?

Being a good actor and being a good auditioner are two totally different skills that require different talents and different parts of your brain. If I could change one thing about acting school curricula, it would be to teach graduating students how to audition. In fact, I think they should focus on audition technique in every year of the program, because it's such a vital element to getting a job. But, like many other actors I know, I learned a lot about acting in school, but I learned very little about auditioning.

So, after four years of school, I moved out West, then spent four additional years learning how to audition. It was really frustrating, I couldn't figure out why I wasn't booking more jobs, after all of my years of training. Sure, I'd get a small role here and there but nothing consistent. Then, finally, I found someone who had the answer: His name is Robert D'Avanzo, and every acting conservatory should pay him top dollar to come and teach at their school. Robert teaches a six-week, on-camera audition class that is the Holy Grail of audition technique. I can't overstate his contribution to my career. *His class saved my life!* See? No overstatement there—it's the truth. I completely credit Robert with changing me from a *good* actor to a *working* actor. After just four weeks in his class, I got twelve callbacks in a row. Twelve! And then I booked a small speaking role on a TV show. Oh my God, my agents flipped out. They were so excited by my momentum that they started sending me out for bigger roles, and I started booking jobs left and right. It was incredible.

How to Practice Auditioning at Home

Here is a simple exercise you can do right now that will help you at future auditions. You will need:

1. A camera that can record video
2. A friend
3. Two chairs

Find a scene from a television show or movie on the internet. (You could also use a play, but a TV show or movie is better for this exercise. The dialogue will be . . . how should I say it . . . more "challenging.") Pretend you have an audition. Work on the scene by yourself. Then, ask a friend to come over and be your "reader." (If you want a real challenge, do not let your friend read the scene until he or she arrives.) Set up the camera so it is only facing and recording you, hit record, have your friend read the other lines, and do the scene.

Watch it back. How do you think you did?

Now, take ten minutes by yourself and make the following adjustments:

1. Memorize the first three lines of the scene so that you don't have to look down at your page.
2. Pick *one* place to have a strong, specific, nonverbal reaction to what the other person is saying.

Now, do the scene again. Did you improve?

The best way to learn how to audition is to practice auditioning. Find scenes, record yourself, watch them back, and make adjustments to your performance. Do this over and over and over. Don't let your real auditions with real casting directors be the only place you practice and perfect your audition technique. Do it at home. Do it now.

Part of Robert's brilliance is that he gives simple, great advice and techniques that actors can immediately apply. For example, one of the little gems that I learned in his class: **You Are Enough**. So often, we worry that we have to bring some amazing razzle dazzle to a role to stand out. We try to figure out what they are "looking for" when really we need to figure out how to bring ourselves to the role. Only you can give your performance. Only you have your unique set of experiences, emotions, and way of expressing yourself. Trust that you are enough.

The Actor's Life

Working a scene with Robert D'Avanzo

The lessons I learned in Robert's class were essential in my landing on *The Office*. When I got the call to audition, I already knew the British version very well. In fact, I thought it was the greatest television comedy ever made. (I still do.) It was very different from anything I'd ever seen on American TV. Very naturalistic, a lot of pauses, and the people look very normal. It looks like a real documentary of a real office. I asked my agent if Allison would be willing to get on the phone with me so I could learn more about what they were hoping to do with the American version of the show. I felt this was appropriate since the role was a lead role, and also since she had been such a champion of mine over the years. (I wouldn't advise asking the casting director to get on the phone with you for a three-line guest role. But I would advise knowing what questions, if any, you should ask once you arrive for that audition.)

Allison agreed to talk with me. I asked her how closely they were planning to mimic the original in style and tone. I wanted to know if this was being played real or if it was being fancied up for American television. She said, "Real! Very real! Don't come in looking pretty!" I was so glad she told me this! A lot of times I was told to look "hot" or "sexy" for a role. I used to get called in to play things like a third-grade school teacher or geriatric nurse and it would say "but look really hot" in the pre-audition notes. (Thus, the red blouse.) Allison told me, "Please look normal, and please do not come in and do a bunch of shtick and try to be funny and clever, because it's not that kind of show. Dare to bore me." Those were her words: *Dare to bore me*. This advice was everything!

When I went into the audition, I did not wear the red blouse. Instead, I wore exactly what I used to wear when I worked in an office—ill-fitting pants, button-down shirt (sort of wrinkled because I didn't really care about my job), and a cardigan (because offices are always cold). I did my hair in ten minutes, letting it dry naturally into a frizz and then pulling it back with a clip (because who gets all dolled up to answer phones?), and I put on virtually no makeup.

> "The first step to a better audition is to give up character and use yourself."
> —Michael Shurtleff

At the audition, I sat in a chair opposite the producer, Greg Daniels. There was a camera behind him, taping my audition. I read the scene and then he wanted me to do some improvisation. He wanted me to act like Pam, or my idea of Pam, while he interviewed me in a documentary-film style. He asked simple questions, such as "How do you like working at a paper company?" and "How long have you lived in Scranton?" and "How do you feel about being filmed by a documentary crew?"

My take on the character of Pam was that she didn't have any media training, so she didn't know how to give a good interview. Also, she didn't care about this interview, because this was some weird project her weird boss was forcing her to do. The first question that they asked was "Do you like working as a receptionist?" I took a long pause and said, "No." And that was it. I didn't speak any more than that. I wanted to stay true to the "dare to bore me" direction Allison had given. They waited for me to say more, and I just didn't. I sat there. They sat there. The silence went on for what felt like an eternity. And then, they started

> "If my career had turned out like the fantasy I had of what it was going to be, it would never have made me happy. But I couldn't have known that until it didn't happen. I found a success that is so much bigger and deeper and better, and it's because it happened later. If *any* of what I'm having happen now—the successes—would have happened to me when I was younger, I would have been ruined. Because when you're young, and things come super easily to you, and you have success right out of the gate, you're liable to think that's how it actually works. You start to think you don't need to be fully prepared or committed to have these things meet you."
> —Sarah Paulson

laughing and asked me a few more questions. I committed to the same tactic. I gave yes and no answers. I felt like the comedy would come in watching me think about what I wasn't going to say, instead of the words that I said. It felt great. Greg and I clicked, and he clearly liked my take on Pam.

Thank God for my audition classes. I really don't know if I'd have been able to nail this audition without having spent the time learning how to audition effectively. I knew how to prepare, I knew what questions to ask, and I knew how to conduct myself in the room because I'd been practicing all these skills weekly in my class. And, I trusted that I was enough.

Again, my teacher's name was Robert D'Avanzo. You can book his class by going to his website, robertdavanzo.com. I recommend the "6-Week On-Camera Audition Class." It's affordable, and the class size is small, which is important because it means each actor gets to perform at every class. If you aren't able to study with Robert, find another good audition class. Practice the process at home. Practice with your friends. Take the time to learn how to audition, because being an effective auditioner is your ticket to becoming a working actor.

The Network Test

The biggest and baddest audition in the world of television is the Network Test. This is a very special final audition you must pass in order

Auditioning, Rejection, and How to Persevere

to be cast as a series regular on a network television show. The term "series regular" refers to a lead character who is set to appear in every episode. When I first moved to Los Angeles, my dream was to land a series regular role on an ensemble comedy show. Playing a defining role on a television series for many years seemed like heaven to me. As you can imagine, the casting of the series regular roles makes or breaks a new show, and so, of course, there is an especially rigorous casting process.

Auditioning to be a series regular starts out the same as any other audition, with pre-reads and callbacks. But then there is a separate producer callback, and maybe even a special work session with the director. At every new stage of the process, you'll notice that the list of actors gets smaller and smaller, until it's eventually whittled down to just two or three people for each role. It's these final two or three people who will "test" for the role. The test is the final step, when the television network executives see you audition and consider you for the role. These people have the final say. The director may love you, the producers may love you, but, to get the job, the network has to love you.

If you are asked to test, your agent will negotiate a seven-year contract with the network. This contract will cover everything: your fee to do the pilot, your episode rate plus yearly pay raises, your trailer size, how and when your name appears in the credits, publicity requirements—literally everything. It can be confusing and overwhelming when this negotiation takes place. A lot of actors get nervous and fear that the negotiation could derail their standing with the network. But you must trust your agents and let them work to get the best deal possible.

When you arrive at your network test, you will be given several copies of your contract to sign *before* you are allowed to audition. If the network picks you for the role, they sign it too. If they don't pick you, the contract is shredded. If you don't have a signed contract, you can't audition.

Most of the time the legal stuff is worked out beforehand, so you don't have to worry about anything except your performance on the day of the audition. It's best to arrive ten to twenty minutes early so you can get the paperwork out of the way, and then have a moment to focus. But if the negotiating is still taking place, try not to fret. My friend just tested for a pilot, and her deal wasn't done when she arrived because her agents were still haggling with the network. The casting director let her go last, to give them an extra half hour to work it out. The negotiation went down to the wire, and she signed the deal mere moments before her audition. She was so incredibly stressed before she went in the room. She had spent the whole time before her audition on the phone with her agents, crying and asking them to please hurry and close her deal! Crazy enough, she got the job.

My network tests were usually in one of two places: a spacious screening room that felt a lot like a small theater, or a cramped conference room with people standing and sitting wherever they can find space. I can't decide which is worse. At least in the conference room I felt like everyone could see my acting. But it's distracting to be performing with someone's nose by your butt. Whatever the venue, the room will be filled with about twenty people—network executives, studio executives, the series director, producers, maybe even some writers. The casting director will be there, too. I found most casting directors went out of their way to be comforting. Remember, casting directors are your advocate; they're rooting for you. Executives, on the other hand, are not so warm and fuzzy. Before my first network test, my agent warned me that executives give off *nothing* at these auditions—no laughter, no reactions, no comments, nothing. It's a strange feeling when you perfectly execute a joke, only to find that the room is silent. But you must trust your choices and trust your performance. Stick with what you've been doing in the previous rounds of auditions; don't make changes unless you're told to. After you've read, they may ask you to read again, or they may not. If they don't, you can always ask if there is anything else they'd like to see.

One time I tested for a new sitcom, a *Friends*-like comedy, and it was between two other girls and me. The role was pretty straightforward: a quirky, dim-witted, sweet best friend. We each went into the room to audition, then were asked to wait in the hallway for the network to make their decision. It was torture; we waited for almost thirty minutes. Then, after what seemed like an eternity, the assistant came out and asked us all to read again. There were no new notes or changes; they simply wanted to see us audition again. So, we each went in, one by one, and read for the network again. After that, we were all excused and went home. The next day I found out that none of us got the part; the creators of the show decided to rework the character. Apparently, they realized through the audition process that the best friend character was very similar to the lead, and they needed to go back to the drawing board. I was of course totally bummed out and figured they were just letting me down easy, trying not to hurt my feelings. But months later I saw the show on the air and, sure enough, the role of the quirky best friend was completely different from what I had auditioned for. She was now a sarcastic, tattooed tough girl.

This is why those testing rooms are so tense and quiet. So much more is happening in the room than just an analysis of your performance. The producers, director, writers, and network executives are seeing their new show on its feet for the first time, and their brains are spinning. They're deciding if the writing is good enough, if the characters are right, if the relationships work. Pretty much everyone in the room is nervous because they all have something at stake. Not just you.

> "I believe this: If an actor wants a role or wants to work with somebody, then you do everything within reason to try to get that role. If they want you to audition, you audition. If they want you to screen-test, you screen-test. If they want you to come and tap-dance in their hallway, you tap-dance in their hallway."
> —Kevin Spacey

My very first test was for a comedy about a group of dancers. The producers made it clear that although the show was about a group of dancers, we'd never really be dancing. They were looking for funny actors with great comic timing, but they wanted people with dance backgrounds so that we'd look believable doing scenes that involved barre work. You might remember my tenure in the dance chorus in high school? That paid off here. I was deemed "dance experienced." I auditioned a billion times for the role: pre-read, callback, producer session, director session, all of it. And then, finally, I got the call: They wanted me to test.

You can imagine how excited I was. This was my first series regular audition, and I had already made it all the way to the network test! I felt confident. I felt ready. I called everyone I knew. I wanted to prepare them for the fact that, very shortly, I would be starring on a hilarious new show about a group of dancers. I was certain everything was about to change.

My agent negotiated the whole test deal. Then, the night before my test, he called and said I needed to arrive early for a dance tryout. But not only that, he also said I would only move on to test if I passed the tryout. What? Are you kidding me?! Oh, and they wanted me to wear a leotard and tights. This was incredibly upsetting; I nearly burst into tears on the phone. "It's 9 PM! Where am I going to get a leotard and tights?" My agent just said, "You have to figure it out." Mind you, this is long before the internet. "Figuring it out" was a lot more difficult than heading to Google. After a mad scramble the following morning, I managed to find a dance store in the Valley that opened at 9 AM. I rushed over to the store and got a leotard, tights, jazz and tap shoes (just in case), then raced to my dance tryout at 10:30 AM. When I arrived at the studio, the room was filled with professional dancers. We lined up and they began to teach us a routine. Not a small, easy couple of steps, but a full routine, very complicated and challenging. This was a far cry from my days of dancing in the mall with my high school dance troupe. After what felt like the most excruciatingly long hour of my life, the teacher signed off on me, meaning I was able to test. I rushed to the bathroom and changed my clothes. Then, moments later, all sweaty and exhausted and drained of emotion, I was taken into the network test. I remember being really nervous, overly friendly, super chatty, and very, very sweaty. I didn't spend much time in the room; it was over very quickly. I could tell when I left that I didn't get the part. The feedback I eventually received was "She danced great, her audition was very funny, but she's just too green." Being "too green" means too inexperienced to handle the pressures of a full-time series regular role. I've always wondered if the dance audition was really a test of my ability to handle the stress and pressure of last-minute changes that happen every day on a professional set. If so, I don't think I passed that test. I was pretty rattled and probably came off like a deer in the headlights. A very chatty deer, mind you. Because that's often what happens when I get really nervous. I can't stop talking.

SURVIVING REJECTION

After the network test for the dance show, I went on to test for roughly six or seven different pilots over the course of three years. It was hard to keep putting myself out there over and over, only to not get the part. But I kept reminding myself what my teacher had told me—that people remember good work. And, sure enough, the same casting director from the dance pilot brought me in the following year to audition for a guest part on a different pilot. It wasn't a series regular, just a one-episode role, playing a secretary to one of the leads. I had one five-line scene in which my character delivered homemade cookies to her boss. My take on the character was that she baked the cookies because she was harboring a secret love for her boss, and maybe these cookies would help him see her as the nurturing woman he needed in his life. Mind you, this wasn't in the script; it was just a backstory I'd created to make my tiny role more interesting. Apparently it worked, because the producers noticed my attention to detail. They said, "We love what you are doing with this cookies thing. What's going on there?" So, I told them my little backstory and they were impressed enough to give me the job. After the shoot, they came up to me and said, "We love your cookie crush thing. And we love the idea of you being this person who is always taking care of him. If the show gets picked up, we want to give you a recurring role." Yay! That was really exciting! Unfortunately, the show didn't get picked up. But it was really cool to have been noticed. (By the way, the key to this little success was that *they asked me* about my character's backstory. I don't recommend you walk into an audition and bother the producers with your little backstory for a three-to-five-line part. If I'd walked in and said, "So, I've got this great idea where I have this crush . . ." they probably would have been like, "Okay, weirdo, just say your five lines and be quiet." And I should point out, if they'd said, "Can you just deliver the cookies and keep it simple?" I'd have said, "Sure!")

> "I always tell actors, when they go in for an audition: Don't be afraid to do what your instincts tell you. You may not get the part, but people will take notice."
> —Robert De Niro

But the story doesn't end there. Five years later, the same guys hired me to play Michael Douglas' daughter in the movie *Solitary Man*. I hadn't seen them since the day of filming on the cookie crush pilot. They literally just called my agent out of the blue and offered me the role, saying, "We've been looking for a way to work with Jenna ever since she played the secretary in our law pilot." Wow. It was the first time I'd ever gotten a role without having to audition. Granted, by this time I was on *The Office*, but it was still about planting seeds from way back: Dance pilot (no) led to cookie crush show (yes, but no pick-up), which led to walking down a Manhattan sidewalk in a scene with Michael Douglas. My teacher was right: "People remember good work."

In addition to talent, training, and hard work, living the life of a working actor requires a very special emotional constitution. You must have a strong will, you must be determined, and you must be able to withstand countless rejections without becoming depressed, cynical, or self-destructive. Because the hard truth is that it often takes more than good work to get the job. It's about doing good work, certainly, but it's also about timing, luck, being the right height, the right weight, having the right hair color, being the right race—any number of arbitrary factors. I have a friend who was flown all the way from New York to Los Angeles to test for a new pilot. It had taken her a month to get to the network test, after numerous pre-reads and callbacks. When she arrived at the studio in Los Angeles, the executives quickly realized that she wasn't right for the role. The reason? She was about four inches taller than the male lead, whom they'd already cast. So, there was no point in moving forward with her. How's that for soul-crushing? Her height could have easily been determined by reading her résumé, and all this could have been avoided. She was sent back to New York without ever having a real chance to compete for the role.

There were so many times I started at the pre-read, clawed my way through countless callbacks, and made it all the way to the test... only to find myself pitted against a name actor. More specifically, Alyson Hannigan. I can't tell you how many jobs I lost to Alyson Hannigan. She had recently finished the series *Buffy the Vampire Slayer* and was a hot commodity. She's also adorable and super funny. Talent and a name—I simply couldn't compete. My feedback was always the same: "We loved Jenna, but we need to go with a name." Why have me audition at all? It was so discouraging.

Certainly, it was great that I was testing for shows. But every time I didn't get the role, I felt like I was right back where I started. I tried to focus on the positives. Casting directors were calling me back, and often they didn't ask me to pre-read because they trusted my work enough to bring me straight to meet the producers. And my agents were excited about me, working hard to get me auditions. Both of these successes didn't exist the year before. So, there were some bright spots. But not as bright as a job, and what I really wanted was a job.

Then, finally, I caught a break. Seven years and what felt like 234,976 auditions later, I booked my first pilot. It was a half-hour comedy called *Rubbing Charlie*, starring Scott Wolf. The show was about a doctor

Me, on the set of my first pilot, Rubbing Charlie, with Scott Wolf's back, which I'm about to rub.

named Charlie (Scott Wolf) and his life coach/massage therapist (me). Thus, *Rubbing Charlie*. (I always thought the name was kind of, well . . . how do I say this? Actually, I think you get it.) We shot the pilot over nine days, and it gave me a first taste of what being a television star could feel like. I had a big trailer filled with all kinds of snacks. I gossiped with the hair and makeup people. I joked with the crew. The producers were supportive and the show was funny. Scott Wolf was grounded and fun to work with. I couldn't wait to spend the next seven years with all these people, making our new hit comedy *Rubbing Charlie*.

Pilots are generally shot in March and April, and then in May the networks announce which shows will be ordered to series. So, there's a little waiting period before you find out if you've struck gold. I wasn't worried; I was sure we had a hit on our hands. I spent those two months frivolously spending my entire paycheck. I took a vacation. I bought an automatic litter box for my cat. And a new couch. Then May arrived, and my dreams were crushed when the network announced their decision: We didn't get picked up. The show was over. I was back to being a poor, unemployed actress.

At this point I was ready to quit. I had worked so long and so hard to finally land a pilot and now I was going to have start all over again next year. I honestly didn't know if I could do it. Sure, I was earning my living as an actor but, like a lot of actors, I wanted a regular job. I was tired of saying three lines here and five lines there, working my butt off every pilot season just to wind up *not* on a TV show again. I was getting so down about my chances that I actually called my agent and manager and told them I wanted to quit the business. I mean, I'd given it *eight years*, which felt like a legitimate amount of time to discover whether or not this was the path for me. I was tired of the rejection. I was tired of feeling like I wasn't enough. I honestly didn't know what more I could do.

My agent reassured me that I was on the right track, pointing out that most actors never even make it to the network test. He told me that it was going to happen eventually; if I just kept at it, the right show would find me. It sounded nice and hopeful, but his speech didn't convince me. And also, it wasn't what I wanted to hear. I wanted someone to tell me that yes, actually, I should quit. So, I called my manager and told her I was done. Surely, she'd get it! Nope. She said, "Jenna, this is what it means to be an actor. So, either you're an actor or you aren't an actor. Are you an actor?" Ugh. She wasn't helping.

So, I called my acting teacher, Robert. Surely he would understand how ridiculous this was, this failing experiment that was wasting my life. I was sure he'd hear my desperation and tell me to pack up and go home to St. Louis. Nope. He yelled at me. He actually yelled, like, angry-yelled at me: "Shut up, Jenna! Stop whining! Stop being a baby! Look how far you've come! How hard you've worked!" Oh my God, Robert gave the exact same speech as my manager, only *way louder*. He continued, "This is what it means to be an actor! This is it! Scrambling for auditions, tons of rejection, and little bits of work in between! You are already doing it! Just keep doing it!" I burst into

> ## Movies about Perseverance
>
> Need a little inspiration to keep you going? Try watching one of these movies:
>
> | | |
> |---|---|
> | *Rocky* | *Erin Brockovich* |
> | *The Edge* (1997) | *The Elephant Man* |
> | *The Mission* | *8 Mile* |
> | *Wild* | *Cast Away* |
> | *The Shawshank Redemption* | *Places in the Heart* |
> | | *The Revenant* |
> | *The Pursuit of Happyness* | |

tears. I said, "You don't get it! I'm tired! It's too hard! All they ever want is name actors. And then when I finally get a pilot, it doesn't get picked up. I can't win!" He yelled more: "Shut up, Jenna! Go work on some scenes and get better!" Like most good coaches, he knew when to push me beyond what I thought were my limits.

I found this Chuck Norris quote and put it on my bathroom mirror: *"A lot of people give up just before they're about to make it. You know, you never know when that next obstacle is going to be the last one."* I defiantly told my representatives that I would give it one more year, and after that I was calling it quits. And, wouldn't you know it, that was the year Allison called me in to audition for *The Office*. Incidentally, here's what it said on the casting notice: **"Unknowns only, NO names."** Isn't that serendipitous? The producers wanted to protect the integrity of the documentary style, casting only unknown actors. They wanted the audience to believe that these were real people in a real office, and they didn't want people to be distracted by celebrity. *Finally*, my lack of success was a *virtue*! Alyson Hannigan would not be auditioning for this role! I tried not to get too excited.

Auditioning, Rejection, and How to Persevere

When it came time to test for *The Office*, they had narrowed it down to four Pams, four Jims, four Dwights, and four Michaels. Rather than have us audition in a conference room, they brought all of us into a real office and filmed us doing scenes on camera for two days, mixing and matching us. It was basically a fully produced screen test, something I'd never done before. The producers told us that the network needed to see how we related to the camera, since that was such a big part of the show.

The morning of my test, I wore the same outfit from my very first audition. I did my hair the same way. I didn't add any makeup even though I knew I would be appearing on camera. I just trusted that my performance was enough. I drove to Culver City and was shown to the second floor of a real office building. I waited in a small office that would eventually become the "break room" on the show. As I sat there, I saw the other Pams. We were all very different types. One of my most vivid memories was that one of the potential Pams was wearing a long skirt with knee-high leather boots. I remember thinking to myself, *Pam would* never *wear those boots!* I kind of became obsessed with her boots: They seemed like such a glaring misread of Pam. I thought, *If that girl gets the part, at the very least they can never let her wear those boots. They just aren't Pam!*

Over the course of those two days, I was asked to read with John Krasinski a lot, which I thought was a good sign because he was definitely the best Jim. I mean, he wasn't just the best Jim—he *was* Jim. I remember the moment we met. As I was being shown to the actor's holding room, he was just being called in to read with another potential Pam (the one with the boots, actually). As he passed by, he introduced himself, and we shook hands. It was as if lightning struck through the center of the room. I knew immediately what was going to happen. John and I were meant to play the flirtatious friends and unrequited lovers, Jim and Pam. I hoped I was right.

The actors didn't talk much in the holding room. I think everyone was very nervous. And I was trying to stay in character. Pam's not very chatty, so I brought a book and read quietly. On the second day, John and I were walking out of an audition scene, and he suddenly turned to me and whispered, "You're my favorite Pam. I hope you get this job." It was exactly as sweet and cute and supportive as anything Jim would say to Pam. I smiled really big and said, "I'm so glad you said that because you're my favorite Jim and I don't think anyone could do it except for you." It gave me a big confidence boost to know we were rooting for each other. When they eventually called to tell me I got the job, the first thing I said—after screaming for joy—was "Please tell me that John Krasinski is playing Jim." And they said, "He is. And, we're so glad to hear you say that, because we thought you two had amazing chemistry, and we're glad you think so, too." I told them I couldn't do Pam without him.

During the testing process, I had heard rumblings that some guy named Rainn Wilson was the favorite to play the office weirdo and Assistant to the Regional Manager Dwight Schrute. But he wasn't in my holding room on the test days. We didn't meet until we were paired up late on the second day of testing. I can honestly say that I've never met a weirder person in my life. Everything he said, the way he stood, the way he was breathing, his hair—it was all so weird! I realized later that Rainn had been staying in character throughout the day, so I was actually meeting and talking with Dwight.

Our audition scene was an improvisation. The producer, Greg Daniels, told Rainn to come up to my desk and talk to me about my fiancé, Roy. He was supposed to suggest all the ways he would make a better boyfriend than Roy. So Dwight (Rainn) approached me and kneeled down very close to my face—like, *very* close—and launched into a long spontaneous monologue about a girlfriend who was fighting in Iraq. He went on and on and on. In addition to naming all the ways he was a great boyfriend, he also talked about some of the ways he could win a knife fight. I didn't say anything. I just listened. I remember thinking about possums, how they freeze when they sense danger. It seemed like this might be Pam's motivation in this bizarre encounter. The less she said, the less she moved, the more quickly this strange man will go away. When it was finally over, I thought it went great. It felt seamless, and I loved working with Rainn. But then they never asked me to audition with him again! I was afraid it was because I had broken character and laughed at one point. But I couldn't help it. He was so funny!

During the final season of *The Office*, the producers found our network test tapes. We all huddled around as a cast and watched them together. It was actually kind of amazing. The casting was crystal clear. The chemistry, the quirks, the humor, we *were* those lovable characters. I couldn't believe it. To think back, all those crazy elements had come together for me—the right timing, right height, right hair color, and a total lack of name value. It was lightning in a bottle.

One of the scenes on those tapes was between me and Steve Carell, who was obviously testing for Office Manager Michael Scott. In the scene, Michael was interrupting Pam's lunch to tell her about his doctor's visit to test for testicular cancer. It was so funny. Steve timed the most uncomfortable details of his story perfectly. Sometimes it was just as I was about to take a bite of my sandwich, sometimes on the swallow, sometimes just as I was raising it to my lips. My favorite was the time you can see me waiting and wondering if it is safe to take a bite: I pause, he pauses, I bite, and he says something gross. I would come to learn this is the brilliance of Steve Carell. Precision. He is a master of comic timing. He hits the bull's-eye every time.

None of us expected the show to take off like it did. After we shot the pilot, we all hugged goodbye, and I handed out scrapbooks; we were expecting to never see one another again. The show just seemed too weird or too different or too *something* to ever make it on the air. Don't get me wrong: We knew it was good. In fact, I was fairly certain it was the very best thing I would ever have the opportunity to do. But never in our wildest dreams did we think we'd get to do it for nearly ten years. Keep in mind, at this point I had been clawing away for eight years, so I knew better than to get my hopes up. And I wasn't alone. Everyone was struggling gig to gig, paycheck to paycheck. Steve got his start with the comedy group The Second City in Chicago. He'd done countless pilots and had been struggling on and off as an actor for almost twenty years. He'd been a regular correspondent on *The Daily Show* and had a memorable scene in the Jim Carrey movie *Bruce Almighty*. He was well respected in the industry but far from a household name. Rainn was a classically trained theater actor. He'd been struggling for fifteen years. He'd done dozens of guest appearances and traveled the country doing theater. But, at that point, his biggest job was a recurring role on the HBO show *Six Feet Under*. John Krasinski had only been out of college for a few years. He had done some commercials and some guest spots, but nothing significant. The supporting cast members all had similar stories. We all needed a break. When we finished the pilot, we were told the network would make a final decision sometime before May 15. I waited for the phone to ring every day for months.

Finally, on May 14 at 7 PM, the network called to say we were picked up. They were ordering five more episodes. We all had jobs.

THE OFFICE - DAY ONE TABLE READ

CHAPTER FIVE
YOU GOT A JOB! HOW THINGS WORK ON A TELEVISION OR FILM SET

> "First of all, I choose the great roles, and if none of those come, I choose the mediocre ones, and if they don't come, I choose the ones that pay the rent."
> —MICHAEL CAINE

No matter how successful you become, there is nothing quite like the moment when you get your first speaking role in film or television. I had been struggling in Los Angeles for five years when it finally happened for me. It was an episode of the television show *Spin City* (when Charlie Sheen was the star), and I played the role of a young lady who worked in a restaurant. Here is what I knew about the character: Her name was Waitress. She wore a white shirt and black pants. In the episode, Charlie Sheen goes on a double date with Heather Locklear, Vanessa Marcil, and Scott Wolf. They go to a restaurant where at one point Vanessa Marcil goes berserk and throws a dinner roll at the Waitress (me).

I had three lines. I'm not sure it's possible for a person to spend more time working on three lines as I did on those for *Spin City*. I remember spending a particularly long time on the line "Is Pepsi okay?" in response to Vanessa's request for a Coke. *Should I start to turn away and then turn back and ask? Should I ask as if I was bored? How would Lisa Kudrow do it?* I went on to create a whole backstory for Waitress: *It's a busy night. I've been working a double shift. My boss is looking over my shoulder.* Ha! All kinds of crazy preparation just to ask about Pepsi and have a dinner roll thrown at my back!

Some things I remember about the shoot:

- It was shot on a studio lot. I had a special drive-on pass, which made me feel important and which I saved in my scrapbook.
- Heather Locklear was strikingly beautiful. And, she talked to everyone. The hair and makeup people loved her.
- Charlie Sheen kept to himself.
- I had never seen so many snack foods in my life. They were everywhere. They even brought a tray of snacks into the hair and makeup trailer while I was getting ready. I pigged out. See ya later, Actor's Pizza!

I remember waiting around *forever* after hair and makeup. I wasn't sure what we were waiting for because no one really updated me. Having nothing else to do, I used the time to snack. After about an hour, the actors were called to set. I was stuffed and nervous, a dangerous combination. Then, just as we were about to start, there was another delay and we had to wait on set. The other actors seemed relaxed and started chatting. I didn't know if I was supposed to talk with them or not. I mean, they were all stars and I was just a day player with three lines. I could hear everything they were saying, even though they were talking amongst themselves. I remember they were discussing a recent story from the tabloids and all the reasons it wasn't true. I couldn't help but eavesdrop; they had such awesome inside information. At some point, I decided to break in and add my own two cents. I quickly regretted this decision. Heather Locklear was very kind; she acknowledged me and drew me in for a sentence or two, and everyone else sort of followed her lead. But it was awkward.

That's when I learned there is a difference between the regular actors and guest actors on a television show. I was like the new girlfriend at a family dinner where everyone starts talking old family gossip. Best not to talk in that situation. Just listen. I stood there, sweating bullets, hoping I wasn't going to get fired or throw up. If only I could have known that in three more years, I'd be rubbing Scott

Wolf's back in a scene for our hit comedy pilot *Rubbing Charlie*. Maybe then I would have felt more confident.

Once we started shooting, everything went by very fast. I said my lines to the director's satisfaction. I kept a respectful distance from the other actors. I ate even more delicious food. And, when the episode aired a month later, all three of my lines made the show.

I learned a few things from that shoot that remain true to this day:

- Most of your day is spent waiting around.
- The most prepared person on a set is the person who has three lines.
- If you are the person with three lines, you are supposed to act like you can't hear what the stars on set are saying around you.
- Sets have lots of food.

So, now it's your turn. Let's pretend you got your first speaking role on a film or television show. First, let me congratulate you. Yay! You did it! You got the job! Congratulations! I assume you've already called your parents and taken a thumbs-up selfie and texted it to all your friends. If you haven't done those things, do them now. *Brag! Celebrate!* This is a big deal! You've been working really hard for this. Just be sure not to mention any details about your new job on social media. Productions are very sensitive about information leaks regarding plots, characters, and shoot locations. I actually know someone who got fired for posting about a new job. She tweeted that she'd booked a great guest spot on a popular television show and then named the actor she'd be working with. The network considered the post a spoiler and recast her. Likewise, when you get to your new job, *no photos.* Can you sneak a selfie in your trailer for your personal scrapbook? Sure. But I wouldn't post it online. And definitely, definitely do not take photos of yourself on set or of the other actors on set. That's a big no-no. And it could land you in serious trouble.

Let's talk about what you can expect going forward, now that you've booked a job. If you've booked a guest role on a television show, there's a good chance you'll start shooting in the next day or two. If you've landed a movie role, you'll probably have a bit longer before reporting to work. This is because movies usually have a longer pre-production period than a TV show. Movies typically shoot over thirty, sixty, or ninety days, as opposed to TV, which is usually a weeklong shoot. In either case, the preparation starts immediately.

TABLE READS

The final table read of The Office

Before shooting begins, you might be invited to attend a "table read." A table read is when the entire cast is assembled in a room filled with studio executives, producers, and writers, and the script is read aloud. Table reads are more common in television shows and big-budget films. Independent, smaller-budget movies may or may not have a table read, simply because they don't have the resources to schedule and pay the actors in advance of the shoot. Television table reads usually happen one week before shooting. On movies, it could be up to a month in advance.

If you're asked to participate in a table read, you'll be reading from the most recent version of the script. You'll most likely be given this draft of the script once you arrive at the reading. Perhaps you've already been working with an earlier draft, highlighting your lines and making notes in the margins. Feel free to arrive early and transfer any of these important details to the new script, should you feel like they would be useful for you in the reading. I always like to arrive early and highlight my lines. But definitely use the script they hand you on the day, not your own from home, because it is very likely that changes have been made.

A table read should sound like the movie or TV show will sound, in terms of the performances. So, despite the fact that you're sitting at a table with a script in your hands, be sure to give as full a vocal performance as possible. Don't just read the words. Be animated. Make the script come alive. Listen to your fellow actors and try to match the energy in the room. Not to make you nervous, but I know people who have been fired after a table read. If the producers feel like something about you or the character is "off," they might fire you and re-imagine things. One of my early jobs was as a replacement for an actor who was let go after a table read. Also, table reads are not the arena for you to try a new take on the character. Do the things that got you the job in the first place. Stay consistent.

I love table reads. They're generally a very positive experience. It's a chance to meet the actors and members of the creative team. The writers get to hear if the dialogue is working and if the arcs in the story make sense. And people laugh at the jokes. We had a table read every single week on *The Office*. Tuesdays, after lunch, we all assembled in the writer's trailer and read the script for the following week. Sometimes our guest actors joined us, sometimes they didn't. If you're not invited to a table read, don't fret—guest roles are often cast after the table read has occurred. This is especially true of smaller roles, because small characters often get altered or cut based on the table read. This was true on *The Office*. Because things would change so much after the table read, they would wait to cast smaller roles until later in the week.

In general, after a table read is over, the actors are dismissed and the director, writers, and producers stay behind to discuss the script. If you have a lingering question, "table" it (aw yeah, a pun). While this might seem like a good time to chat up the director and ask your question, it's actually not. You should exit with the other actors.

WARDROBE

Shortly after you get the good news from your agent, you'll start getting phone calls from various members of the production team. You probably think your first call might be from the director or producer, but it's usually from someone in the wardrobe department. Once I even found out about a job because the wardrobe person called me and started asking me questions. My agent called to tell me I'd booked the job, thirty minutes later. Crazy, right? Wardrobe will need to know your clothing sizes and may even want to set a wardrobe fitting with you before you start work. When they ask your sizes, *tell the truth*. If you are somewhere between a medium and large, tell them this. Don't just say "medium." And don't tell them what size you hope to be by the time you start shooting. Tell them the size you are now. There is nothing more embarrassing than getting to a fitting where everything is too small because you didn't want to admit your real sizes. Most wardrobe departments have a tailor on hand to make things smaller. But they can't make stuff bigger.

Be prepared to bring your own clothes. Even though it's a SAG-AFTRA job, and you've entered the big time, it's possible you'll still have to wear your own stuff. In fact, I think every actor (male and female) should own a business suit that fits them well. If you are playing a lawyer, real estate agent, or business executive, there's a good chance you will be asked to bring a suit to the fitting. And there are certain things I bring to every fitting, even if they don't ask. I always bring a nude bra, black bra, nude undies, black undies, and a thong. You never know what you might be asked to wear, and having undergarments that fit well are important. I also think it is a good idea, especially for women, to bring a few pairs of your own shoes. The last thing you want to do is get stuck standing in uncomfortable shoes all day. Finally, I like to bring my favorite pair of jeans. Finding a great-fitting pair of jeans is not easy, as we all know. When you're only working one or two days on a project, the wardrobe department doesn't have time to search high and low for the perfect pair of jeans for you. Even now it's still the same: I recently did a one-day guest role on a TV show; I brought my own jeans to the fitting and ended up wearing them on the show.

At most fittings, a wardrobe person and several assistants watch as you undress and try on various outfits. Everyone talks about what fits, what's flattering, and what isn't. It can be a little unnerving, especially for a modest person who doesn't love getting undressed in front of other people, like me. I often ask for privacy to change, especially if an outfit requires me to remove or change my bra or underwear. It's totally okay to ask people to leave while you change.

Your fitting will likely feel rushed. This is normal, as everyone on set is always in a time crunch. That said, it's perfectly acceptable for you to have reasonable opinions about the clothes you are wearing. If you feel like something is unflattering or not your character, say so. I'll say something like, "This wouldn't be my first choice." Or, "I don't love this one." Sometimes I still end up wearing things that don't quite feel right, but I try to speak up if I really hate something. Ultimately, you are the one in front of the camera, so make sure that you feel comfortable. The last thing you want is to be distracted by some element of your wardrobe while you're trying to act.

You Got a Job! How Things Work on a Set

If you've ever wondered why actors seem to obsess about their weight it is because of the dreaded fitting. Your size is not a private affair. My manager has my sizes on file in her office. Height, weight, pant, dress, bra, waist, hip, and shoe are all standard requests. When I book a job, she forwards my sizes to the wardrobe department and someone shops for my costumes based on this information. In a normal job, if you gain or lose a few pounds, it's no big deal. Just grab your "fat jeans" and blousy top and vow to get to the gym more often. But in this business you have to tell someone you've gained weight so that the next time you go to a fitting, the clothes are the right size. Take, for example, the email I send to my manager after every holiday season: "Happy New Year, Naomi! Just wanted you to know I enjoyed the holidays, including lots of my mom's snowball cookies. I'm now a size 6 pant instead of a 4. Talk soon!" Emails go out to the agents, stylists, and wardrobe department: "Jenna would like everyone to know that she's now a 6 pant." Such fun!

When I was on *The Office*, Pam had her own "closet" in the wardrobe office. It was filled with pencil skirts, button-down tops, and cardigans. Each week the wardrobe department would pull a skirt, top, and sweater for me to wear. If my sizes suddenly changed, nothing would fit. Luckily, they knew me and my sweet tooth. They kept a few bigger skirts on hand so I'd have something to wear after Christmas break.

> "I think the most liberating thing I did early on was to free myself from any concern with my looks as they pertained to my work."
> —Meryl Streep

My character in the film *Walk Hard* had something like ninety different costumes, many of which were skimpy lingerie. Before the shoot, the studio hired a personal trainer and nutritionist, who promptly put me on a very strict diet and exercise plan. Since movies shoot their scenes out of sequence, I had to stay the same size for the duration of the shoot, so that my character looked consistent. The slightest change in my weight could throw off all the continuity. This was the first time I'd experienced my figure being such an essential element to a character. It was fun. I was being paid to work out. I mean, it was my *job* to have a rockin' bod. By the time we were ready to start shooting, I was in the best shape of my life. I can't really take credit: If you cut out sugar, caffeine, bread, complex carbs, saturated fats, dessert, and alcohol and train two hours a day, six days a week, for three months, it's impossible not to look pretty amazing. My wardrobe fit me perfectly. One of my costumes was a custom-made horse-riding outfit with hand-sewn sequins and beading. It was spectacular.

About three quarters of the way through the shoot, I hit a wall. I was so sick of eating quinoa and grilled chicken and steamed vegetables—every meal was so boring. Oh, and berries for dessert. (I'd just like to say, berries are not a dessert. I'm happy to eat them, but don't tell me they're dessert. Just tell me I'm eating chicken, quinoa, vegetables, a *side* of berries, and *nothing* for dessert.) Anyway, where was I? Oh yes, we're about three quarters of the way through the shoot, we are shooting on location, I'm staying in a hotel in the desert, it's late at night, and I'm *starving*. I peruse the boring pre-packaged microwave meal from my nutritionist, and I realize I can't put another lump of gray, grilled chicken into my mouth. I stare at the room service menu. Should I do it? I figure, the shoot's almost over. And it's only one meal, right? I'll go back to bland city tomorrow. So, I text my co-star Chris Parnell: "Hey, do you want to get burgers from room service and watch a movie?" His text back was the greatest I've ever received: "Sure." I pick up the phone and order a giant cheeseburger with fries, wine, and a Diet Coke. (Yes, I ordered wine *and* Diet Coke.) I might have also ordered an ice cream sundae for dessert. Or two.

I get to work the next day and realize we're shooting the horse-riding scene, the one with the tight-fitting *custom riding outfit*. Oh, no. I walk in my trailer and there it is, in all its beaded glory, taunting and daring me to try it on. So, I put on the pants. Well, sort of put on the pants, because they won't zip. I'm not kidding. They will not zip up. It's like I gained five pounds overnight. My body must have been so excited to have real food, it decided to save it to my hips immediately. I called the wardrobe woman into my trailer. "What happened?!" she said. "I ate a burger," I said, sheepishly. "Okay, don't worry," she said. "I'll find something." She dug around and came back with a generic black riding outfit. As she handed it to me, I could tell she was heartbroken. It wasn't nearly as cool as the custom one.

When I walked on set, the director had to be told about the wardrobe change, as he had approved the original outfit. I was so embarrassed. And then there's the woman who sewed the custom one, who wouldn't get to see her handiwork on screen anymore. All because I ate a burger. No wonder so many actors and models have eating disorders. Your size and weight are constantly on display, constantly being scrutinized. It can be very stressful, not to mention shameful.

Luckily, I'm not often cast in roles that require me to wear a bikini. And I don't have food issues. I eat regular meals and real desserts (not berries). But that doesn't mean I don't also feel pressure to stay in good

Here I am, post-burger, in my non-custom riding outfit for the movie Walk Hard.

physical shape and maintain a consistent size. It's not about being tiny. The point is, whatever your size, you want to stay consistent—at least for the duration of whatever role/project you are working on. If you take on a role with certain physical requirements, make sure you can realistically maintain them for the entire shoot. Resist the temptation to pack on pounds, yo-yo diet, and do crazy cleanses. It's not healthy. Your body is your instrument. You need to treat it kindly. People come in all shapes and sizes, and so do characters. Embrace a healthy size that feels easy to maintain and go from there.

PROPS, EATING, AND SMOKING

If your character has to eat food in a scene, the props department will be the people in charge of providing the food. They may call and ask if you have any food allergies. Obviously, tell the truth. If you have a major food aversion, like you vomit every time you smell salmon, be honest and tell them. I'm sure you really don't want to throw up on set, and they don't want you to, either. Even if the scene calls for salmon, they can develop something else that will work.

When you shoot a scene, you don't just do it once. It takes hours, over and over, from different angles to shoot a scene. If you have a scene at a dinner table, you won't just have to eat dinner once, you'll have to eat dinner all day. So, if props gives you a food choice, ask for something *light*. Keep in mind that they'll serve you cooked food, but chilled. If you're having chicken parmesan, it will be fully cooked but served cold so that it won't go bad under the hot lights. Keep this in mind. Only eat when absolutely necessary.

I remember the first time I was asked what I'd like to eat in a scene. We were shooting on location at a restaurant. They gave me a menu and told me to pick a meal. There was steak on the menu. I was a starving artist so I sheepishly said, "Steak and potatoes?" They said, "Sure thing!" I was so excited. Not only did I have a job, but I was going to eat free steak. Cut to hour eight of me eating cold steak and potatoes: Oh my God, I was so sick. And so full. Now, I order salad or penne pasta. Never ever, ever, ever steak again.

This reminds me of the time on *The Office* when the cast had to eat mint chocolate chip ice cream cake. In Season One we had an episode called "The Alliance," where Michael forces the party planning committee to plan a birthday party for Meredith. He then instructs them to serve mint chocolate chip ice cream cake, disregarding the fact that Meredith is lactose intolerant, because it's his favorite cake.

So, on the day, we started filming the party scenes around 7:30 AM. Mindy Kaling and I were in the background of the scene, very excited to be eating cake at work, especially mint chocolate chip ice cream cake. We were taking huge bites, one after the other, basically stuffing our faces. Steve Carell saw us and offered a warning: "Guys, you may want to ease up on the cake. Maybe fake it a few times. Especially because you're in the background. You don't want to get sick." Did Mindy and I pay attention to this sound advice? Nope! We just kept shoveling mint chocolate chip ice cream cake into our faces.

By 9 AM I was bouncing off the walls with a sugar high, laughing hysterically and ruining takes. I must have been so annoying to everyone in the cast. Then, at lunchtime, I started crashing. I was so full of that minty cake, I couldn't eat any real food. I started to feel sick and lay down in my trailer. But after a few minutes, I was called back to set. By now I was feeling totally queasy and close to crying, and I swore in the future I would always pretend to eat food when I was in the background of a scene. I walked on set and realized there were more cake scenes to shoot. Only now, instead of being in the background, it was time for my close ups, which meant I couldn't pretend to eat the cake—I had to devour it. Just holding the plate of cake made my stomach turn. I didn't know it was possible to hate cake as much as I now hated mint chocolate chip ice cream cake. I was gagging every take.

At 6 PM, the day was finally over. I went home and went to bed, feeling bloated and disgusting. The next morning, I got to work, ready to move on from yesterday's debacle. Well, guess what I was handed when I walked on set? *Another piece of mint chocolate chip ice cream cake.* Yep. It took us two full days to shoot the party scenes. Two days of that awful mint chocolate chip ice cream cake. If you watch the episode, you barely see anyone eating cake—it all ended up on the cutting room floor. Hilarious. I ate all that cake and it never even made it into the episode. And now I hate ice cream cake.

I recently asked Angela Kinsey, who played Angela, how she got through those days of shooting the birthday cake scenes. She told me that she and Phyllis Smith, who played Phyllis, had a bucket under one of the desks, and at the end of every take they would spit any unswallowed cake into the bucket. These buckets are actually common in scenes that require eating. They're called "spit buckets," and I don't know why I didn't use one in the scene. If you have a scene with lots of "eating," I suggest you be like Angela and Phyllis and look for the spit bucket.

The same logic that applies to picking your meal applies to scenes that require smoking. If you don't have to smoke in a scene, I wouldn't volunteer to do so. Smoking even an herbal cigarette becomes difficult after eight hours.

FREE FOOD

If you couldn't tell already, I like food. If you ask me, the best part of booking an acting gig when you are a starving artist is the free food. (As long as it's not mint chocolate chip ice cream cake.)

There are two ways to get food on set: Catering and Craft Services. Meals are provided by Catering; Craft Services or "Crafty" means snacks.

Grabbing cake from the Craft Services table during the taping of the "Dinner Party" episode of The Office

There are usually two hot catered meals provided each day by Catering: breakfast (meal upon arrival) and lunch. If you arrive first thing in the morning, a production assistant will ask you for a breakfast order. You can order pretty much anything you want. My favorite is two scrambled eggs with a side of turkey bacon (if they have it), a bowl of fruit, and coffee with milk. Don't be afraid to ask for food. It's part of the SAG-AFTRA agreement; they have to feed you. If you are on a lower-budget production they may direct you to a buffet, which will usually have things such as oatmeal, cold cereals, bagels, muffins, eggs, juice, and coffee. If you are on a super duper low-budget production, all bets are off. You might just get a plate of muffins.

"Lunch" is served six hours after Crew Call. Crew Call is the time that the crew arrives to set. Actors are usually told to arrive before the crew, to go through hair and makeup. So, quick math: If you arrive at 5:30 AM, but the crew arrives at 7 AM, then lunch is at 1 PM. But, let's

Me and Oliver Hudson enjoying lunch on the set of Splitting Up Together

say you're doing a midday shoot and the crew arrives at noon. Lunch is at 6 PM. Even though it's being served at 6 PM, everyone will call it "lunch."

If you hear someone talking about "Crafty," they're talking about the snack table. Crafty is usually located close to set and has coffee, water, soft drinks, fruit, nuts, gum, and other little treats. If it's a big-budget production, it may have hot food options, too. On *The Office*, our Craft Services department served a hot snack twice a day. Sometimes the hot snack was as big as a meal. They would serve tacos, hot dogs, pasta, Thai food, homemade soup . . . they really went all out. On low-budget projects, Craft Services is probably a bunch of bananas and a bowl of cashews. But, the point is, if you need something to munch on, just ask for Craft Services. If you are an extra, you are generally not allowed to eat off the Craft Services table. This is reserved for the crew and union actors with speaking roles.

If you have special dietary needs (gluten free, vegetarian, food allergies), consider packing your own food just in case they don't have what you need.

PREPARATION AND THE NIGHT BEFORE

The night before you're scheduled to work, a member of the production team will call and communicate your "call time," or arrival time, for the next day. You will also be provided directions to the set, instructions on where to park, and what scenes you'll be doing that day. Most of the time you won't receive this phone call until the end of the production's work day, which is usually anywhere from 7 to 10 PM.

Hopefully, you've already been sent a script. If not, ask the caller how you can get your hands on one. This is also a good time to ask if there have been any changes made to the script. It's not unusual to receive new script pages, with all new dialogue, the night before or upon your arrival the next morning. In fact, each morning when you arrive on set, they'll hand you a small packet of papers called "sides." Remember those from your auditions? The sides they hand you on set include the most updated version of each scene that's being shot on that day, as well as the day's schedule. Read the sides. Don't assume they match the script you were sent earlier.

Changes can, and do, happen all the time. I recently did a guest appearance on a television show playing a doctor specializing in Alzheimer's disease. In one scene, I had to deliver a three-page speech to a board room full of people, a long monologue that included all sorts of complicated medical jargon and statistics. I spent an entire week working on it, perfecting my lines

> "I've always considered myself to be just average talent and what I have is a ridiculous insane obsessiveness for practice and preparation."
> —Will Smith

and performance. When I showed up on set, I started joking with the assistant director about how prepared I was, telling him I'd nail the whole thing in a couple of takes. He was very happy to hear this, because it meant he'd make up for time lost earlier in the day. Then the director approached and asked if I wanted a rehearsal. I jokingly scoffed and said he should shoot the rehearsal, because I was ready to go. He was thrilled and we all got into position. We started rolling and I launched into my epic medical monologue. I got a few lines in and the director stopped me and asked if I was joking. I laughed and said no. I figured he was messing with me after I was so overconfident moments before. He then told me something was wrong because I was doing the wrong script. I laughed again, but then got a little nervous when he wasn't laughing back. A long silence followed as the director and assistant director whispered to each other. Finally, the director looked up at me and asked if I got the new script, the one that was sent a few days before. Uh, no. He went on to apologize, saying they had to rewrite the entire monologue for legal reasons, then proceeded to hand me brand new pages. I read silently over the new pages and was horrified. It was an all-new speech. And here I had been bragging about how prepared I was, when in fact I was completely in the dark. I freaked out and apologized, saying it was my fault; I must not have looked at the new pages they had sent out, or the sides today, because I was so overconfident. Long silence as everybody looked around the room. I then said, if they could give me a quiet space for thirty minutes, I could memorize the new script and be ready. And, thanks to my training, I was able to do pretty well. The director also suggested we shoot the speech in sections, which was helpful, but also cost valuable time on a day when we didn't have much to spare. This entire embarrassing fiasco could have been avoided if I'd just read the latest script and prepared properly.

It's not easy to navigate all the changes and keep your focus. And this is just the beginning. It's not just scripts that change. Schedules change, too. Almost every time I book a job, I find out around 8 PM that I need to report the following day at 6 AM. Totally normal. Also, totally stressful. I used to think, *How am I supposed to know what to prepare when I find out so late the night before?* The best approach is to have all your work ready to go, no matter what. Something to know about film sets is that things are always changing at the last minute. They might tell you, "Tomorrow we are shooting Scene 16 at the carnival," but you get to the set, find out that someone is sick, or they lost a location, or it's raining . . . and now you need to shoot the indoor kitchen scenes instead. I remember once I was expecting to work in a scene where I only had one or two lines. I wasn't concerned at all; it seemed like an easy day at work. But when I arrived, I was told that the lead actor of those scenes was sick and not able to come to work, so they had decided to shoot one of my scenes that was scheduled for later in the week. It was a scene with tons of dialogue. I sort of knew my lines but hadn't really fine-tuned my performance. I panicked and started cramming right away. Luckily, by the time they called me to the set for the scene, I was ready. Now, I make sure I have my whole role fully prepared on day one, and I read every script and every set of sides each morning so I'm ready for anything.

THE WORK DAY BEGINS: YOUR ARRIVAL

A typical day of shooting usually lasts twelve to fourteen hours and begins around 6 AM, meaning you have to *be there* at 6 AM. You should plan to arrive showered, with no makeup and clean hair. You might want to blow dry/style your hair the way you like it. If you have a smaller role, the stylist probably won't spend a lot of time on you (unless it is a period piece or there is a specific hair reference in the script). Men, if you auditioned with facial hair, arrive with facial hair. Otherwise, arrive clean shaven. If you forget, the makeup department

Early morning in the hair and makeup trailer on The Office

will give you a razor and shaving cream. But, they aren't the best razors, so better to shave at home.

Allow a lot of extra time to get to the set and park. I find that about 70 percent of the time some portion of the directions I've been given are incorrect. If I'm shooting on a studio lot, about 50 percent of the time my name isn't at the gate as promised, and I have to wait while they call someone to verify my entrance. Sometimes the parking is very far from the set and requires a shuttle to take you from parking to your trailer at "base camp." Build in time for traffic, wrong directions, confusing signs, and a long walk/van ride from parking to base. Your call time is the time you are expected to land at base camp, not the time you park your car. Keep that in mind.

Each day a production report is written up and sent to the studio, listing all of the hiccups from the set on that particular day. You don't want your name on that report. If you're late, it goes on the report as "talent was late," no matter what the circumstances. It won't say "talent was late because we failed to give them accurate directions, sent them thirty minutes out of their way, and then forgot to leave their name at the gate." It just says "talent was late."

When you arrive at base camp, you will most likely be greeted by a PA (Production Assistant). If you aren't, find one and introduce yourself. PAs are the people running around with little headsets in their ears like they're Secret Service. Make sure they know you have a speaking role and are not an extra. I can't tell you how many guest actors wind up in the extras holding area because they're too shy to explain they have a speaking role that day. The PA will show you to your trailer and give you a moment to get settled.

If you have a SAG speaking role in a TV show or movie—no matter the size of the role—you get a trailer or private dressing room. In general, the size of your trailer is directly proportional to the size of your role. Most day players get placed in a "honeywagon," which is a trailer divided into five private dressing rooms. This will be a teeny tiny room, but it's all yours, so enjoy!

A typical Hollywood trailer. So glam. So incredibly glam.

If you are working on a SAG low-budget movie, they're not obligated to give you a trailer or private room. You may be placed in a group holding area/green room instead. However, you must be provided with a private place to change clothes.

After showing you to your trailer, the PA will likely present you with tax forms and a hard copy of your contract to sign. You will want to come prepared with your driver's license and Social Security card or passport. You will need to complete these forms before you are allowed to step on set. Next, you will be taken to the wardrobe department, especially if you haven't already had a fitting. After your wardrobe meeting, it'll be on to hair and makeup, then back to your trailer to sit and wait until they're ready for your scene. You might wait one hour; you might wait five hours; you might wait ten. When I was working on the film *Blades of Glory*, there was a day I waited in my trailer for twelve hours, only to be sent home because they never got to my scene. I just sat there, all dolled up in my full hair, makeup, and wardrobe, waiting.

Playing a little basketball between scenes on the set of The Office

Actors hate waiting. It's boring and it drains your energy and momentum. Not to mention, the anticipation makes it hard to really relax. I've tried reading. I've tried writing. I've tried scrapbooking. None of it really works. I'm constantly distracted, wondering when they're going to knock on my door and tell me they're ready. I feel like I'm a boxer waiting for the bell to ring. I try to look at my lines or study my scene. Sometimes I return emails. But, mostly, I wind up sitting there with a weird combination of bored anticipation.

There's a famous saying among actors in the movie business: "They pay me to wait; I do the acting for free." It's true, because the excruciating part of the job is the waiting. It feels like torture. Unless, of course, you're lucky enough to get a big tricked-out trailer like I had on *Blades of Glory*. For some reason on that film I had a giant full-sized trailer with a mini kitchen, wraparound leather couch, and cable TV. I didn't personally ask for this amazing perk; I'm assuming I had it because my agents did a fantastic job negotiating for me. So, the waiting was bearable, to say the least. I was basically paid to sit and channel surf all day. But, most of the time, you won't have that trailer. And, neither will I. Most of the time I have a reasonably comfortable, cable-free, no WiFi, cold little room to sit in while I wait. And, it's pretty boring.

If you plan on leaving your trailer for any reason—let's say, to get a snack, which is totally acceptable—be sure to tell a PA. Find the one that greeted you, or one of the many other PAs on the set. No matter what, be sure someone knows where you are at all times. If you would like a bottle of water, ask the PA. If you need a copy of the sides, ask the PA. If you want to know how to operate the air conditioner or heat in your trailer, ask the PA. You can ask your PA pretty much anything. But a word of advice: The PAs woke up before you, run around all day, eat lunch standing up, and leave well after you. They are the hardest-working, lowest-paid person on the set. Be kind to them.

ON SET

When you are finally called to set, the first thing you'll do is rehearse. This might be the first time you're meeting the other actors (unless you ran into them at the table read or in the hair and makeup trailer). During rehearsal, everyone holds their sides and reads the scene aloud. After that, you'll start to block it out and get a sense of the movement in the scene. No one expects you to perform the scene at full speed at this point, so don't expect to be given any notes on your acting. This rehearsal is not about your acting performance; it's all about logistics. The director and DP (director of photography) want to figure out where everyone is sitting, standing, walking, moving,

On the set of The Office, *rehearsing a scene for director Lee Kirk and DP Matt Sohn*

entering, or exiting. It goes quickly. Then, once you set the blocking, they invite the crew to watch a rehearsal. Again, this is really just for logistics. The crew is watching to see where they should set the camera, lights, and sound equipment, so don't feel like you need to perform. After all this, the cast is dismissed.

Depending on how long the crew needs to set up, you will either be sent back to your trailer or asked to stay in the cast holding area (a collection of director's chairs on set). Setting of the camera and lights lasts anywhere from fifteen minutes to forty-five minutes on a TV show. On a movie, it can take several hours. So, it's more waiting. I usually walk over to the snack table and peruse the offerings. During this time the periphery crew will do their work: The sound people will come over and put a microphone on you; the props people will ask which briefcase you want to carry or which watch you want to wear, and so on. Then, once the lighting is done, they'll call you back to the set. You'll usually do one more rehearsal before shooting begins, but this time it will be "for camera." This final rehearsal is generally done without scripts and everyone tries to do it with the same energy as a real take. It will likely be your only real rehearsal of the scene before you start shooting.

Next, you will hear someone shout "last looks," which is the signal for the hair, makeup, and wardrobe people to swoop in and touch you up. Once they're done, finally, you will do a take. So, from the time you arrived on set, it's probably around three to four hours before you actually start acting on camera. Crazy, right?

On average, you get about four to five takes. That's four to five chances to nail your performance. Many times, a take doesn't work because of a sound issue or a camera issue, so it's important that your performance remain consistent. Getting a great take is a delicate dance between the actors and camera and sound departments. Every element has to work. That said, don't put pressure on yourself to do the entire scene exactly perfect every time. As long as you get a good read on each line at least once, the editor can piece together a good performance. That's the benefit of film and television: It's not live.

A general rule for actors is that you should never stop the scene for any reason, especially if you are not one of the leads. Only the director stops the scene. If something obvious happens—if you start choking or someone has a sneezing fit—please, by all means, stop acting. I remember once on *The Office*, I was in the middle of a scene with John Krasinski, when a lighting gel slowly peeled off above me and landed on top of my head. Now, clearly, we couldn't continue this scene, so it made sense for me to break. But, if you or another actor flubs a line or if you hear a phone ring off camera, don't stop. Keep going until you hear the director yell "cut." You'd be surprised how

"Last looks" on the set of Rubbing Charlie

You Got a Job! How Things Work on a Set

Waiting to shoot a scene with Steve Carell

these "distractions" or "mistakes" can bring about a new and interesting element of the performance. Always keep going.

When the director feels like you've gotten the scene, you will take a short break while they move the cameras for another angle. Not to sound like a broken record, but I find these breaks are a great time to see what new snacks are on the snack table. You never know what new item may have suddenly appeared.

When the lighting break is over, the whole process starts over again, until all the shots in that scene are complete. Eventually, you'll hear the assistant director yell "Cut! Moving on!" This means they are ready to move to the next scene of the day. If you're in it, you will go immediately to rehearse. If you aren't, you'll be sent back to your trailer to wait.

And that's your day: Arrive, eat, wardrobe, hair/makeup, wait, rehearse, wait/snack/shoot, wait/snack/shoot, wait/snack/shoot, wrap. When I told my actor friend that I was writing this section of the book, she said, "Oh, be sure to tell everyone that a typical shooting day is really slow and boring; you will wait around for hours, and then when it's time to act, everything will move super fast. And then it'll be over and you'll feel like you've got no idea what just happened." This made me laugh. It's just so true.

MULTI-CAMERA TELEVISION

What I just described was a typical work day on a movie or a single-camera television show, like *The Office*. Things work differently on a multi-cam television show. This type of show is rehearsed like a play, then taped and performed in front of a live studio audience. An example of a three-camera comedy would be *The Big Bang Theory* or *Everybody Loves Raymond*. These are a rare breed nowadays, but they still exist. Their schedule looks something like this:

Monday: Table read, wardrobe fittings, hair and makeup test
Tuesday: Rehearsals and blocking with director
Wednesday/Thursday: More rehearsals, including run-throughs for the writers and studio executives. If scenes need to be pre-taped, they happen on Thursday.
Friday: Tape day. You arrive around noon, do a final rehearsal, eat "lunch," and then tape in front of a live audience that evening.

I've done a few guest appearances on three-camera comedies and the schedule can't be beat. Rehearsal days usually start around 10 AM and are over by 5 PM. It's the perfect job if you have a family and want to drop your kids off at school and be home to serve them dinner. Throughout the week you receive re-writes of the script based on your rehearsals. I love this. It's fun. It feels very collaborative. If they are rehearsing a scene you aren't in, there are chairs nearby where everyone sits and watches. On film sets if you aren't in a scene you are stuck waiting in some hallway or in your trailer. It's way more fun to watch other actors working than it is to stare at your trailer walls.

When I did my gig on *Spin City*, they pre-taped my restaurant scene. Even though the show was mostly filmed in front of an audience, they occasionally shoot scenes without an audience, mostly due to scheduling issues or set requirements. On my day, we rehearsed and then shot the scene in a matter of a few hours. But I've had other roles on three-camera shows in which I rehearsed throughout the week and shot in front of an audience. It was exhilarating. A great gig if you can get it.

LOVE SCENES AND FIGHTS

Someone once told me the best reason to become an actor is so you can "kiss people and shoot guns with no consequences." I've done both things on camera and I find they produce a strikingly similar experience. In both cases, my palms get sweaty, my heart races, and I wind up feeling a little jazzed afterward.

If you get cast in a role that requires doing stunts or love scenes, don't worry. Unlike regular scenes where you rush through the rehearsals, most of the time these types of scenes get special rehearsals and lots of planning. Especially stunts. For insurance and safety purposes, studios have to be especially careful about any scenes involving actors and stunt work. There will be a safety officer, a stunt coordinator, and a medic standing by at all times. Even something simple, like a shove against a wall or a slap across the face, requires elaborate planning to make sure no one gets hurt.

I recently did a role where my character had to run into the street to stop a moving car that is barreling toward her. Then, when the driver won't give her a ride, she shoots him and takes the car. So, not only did the scene require me to run into traffic, I also had to shoot a gun. Needless to say, we rehearsed this over and over and over again. The driver of the car was a trained stunt driver. But even after all the rehearsal and the confidence of knowing I was working with a professional driver, I couldn't help but flinch and step backward every time the car got close. It just felt like he wasn't going to stop in time. He did, but it was still pretty scary.

Any time a weapon, such as a gun, is used in a scene, things get serious. Before being given my prop gun (which was actually a real gun loaded with blanks), I received training on how to fire and handle the gun by an on-set weapons specialist. I learned about the kick-back involved with firing a handgun and wore tiny flesh-colored earplugs to make sure the sound did not damage my ears. Even though I was firing a blank, it felt and sounded real. As soon as the director yelled "cut" the weapons specialist came over and took the gun from me. I wasn't allowed to carry it around or play with it when we weren't shooting, which was fine by me. Great care was taken to make sure everyone remained safe.

Love scenes also require special preparation. However, just because you have more elaborate rehearsals, they still tend to happen on the day you shoot the scene. It is very possible that you will shake hands with your co-star, say "nice to meet you," and then begin planning an intimate make-out session. A few things you should know about love scenes:

- No one expects you to kiss for real during rehearsal. As you block out the love scene, it is customary to mime the kissing parts until the camera is rolling.
- Most of the time, especially on TV, you can get away with "stage kissing": You open your mouth but keep your tongue to yourself. Unless the scene clearly calls for something more intimate, stage kissing will usually suffice. That being said, it's customary to brush your teeth and swish some mouthwash before shooting. Or at the very least, chew some minty gum.
- I've heard of some actors who use love scenes as an opportunity to informally cheat on their significant others. This is usually in the form of "private rehearsals" in a trailer. If this offer is made to you, don't be fooled: If you aren't on set with the director, it's not really a rehearsal.
- Nudity in a scene is something that is disclosed and agreed to *before* you take on a role. A director or producer should never suddenly pressure you while on set into taking off your clothes. If this is happening to you, calmly excuse yourself and call your agent or SAG representative immediately. I have a "no nudity" clause in all of my contracts. You can ask for this agreement as well. Nudity clauses are very specific and deal with how much, if any, nudity you will allow. I've heard of actors with nudity clauses that say things like "actor will show top of ass, but not full ass" or "actress will show side of boob, but not

nipple." How's that for specific? Mine says "no nudity" so no top of ass or side boob from me.
- Don't be embarrassed if you get a little excited during a love scene. Even though you are playing a character, your body may not know you are pretending. You may want to plan ahead for some "wind down" time after the scene. There is a good chance your adrenaline will be pumping. Do some yoga, drink some tea, and re-center yourself.

No matter whom the scene is with, most likely the other actor is just as nervous as you are. It's a weird and unnatural thing to pretend to be intimate with someone, who more than likely, for various reasons—for example, you are both in relationships with other people—you would not be intimate with in real life. So, relax, they probably feel as freaked out as you do.

My first big on-camera kissing scene was with John Krasinski, when we filmed Jim and Pam's first kiss on *The Office*. In case you aren't familiar with the show, Jim and Pam were co-workers who had been flirting for two seasons. In addition to being my first big onscreen kiss, this was their first kiss, and everyone on the show wanted to get it just right.

The writers decided the kiss should take place after a casino-themed work party. In the episode, Jim confronted Pam in the parking lot and told her that he loved her. Pam, feeling guilty for being engaged to someone else, told him that she only thought of him as a friend. Jim was broken-hearted and left. Pam, equally broken-hearted, went back inside and called her mom, confessing her feelings for Jim. Suddenly, Jim entered the office, walked over to Pam, and kissed her. She didn't hesitate and immediately kissed him back. This was obviously a big moment, and it proved what all viewers knew—that Jim and Pam were meant to be together.

In the weeks prior to shooting, John and I had long discussions with our director Ken Kwapis, the writers, and producer Greg Daniels.

I also had private conversations with Ken about how I thought Pam might be feeling in the moments before the kiss, and how she might react afterward. We did a lot of prep work. But we didn't officially rehearse the scene until the day of the shoot.

The kissing scene was scheduled for the end of our work week, later in the evening, after most people were sent home. Only a small crew and a few writers and producers remained. Ken recently told me, "I remember that you and John were off-the-charts nervous, and I felt it was my job to be as casual about the scene as possible, to undercut how momentous I knew it was. It didn't help matters that, on the shooting schedule, the scene description read as follows: '*JIM KISSES PAM!!!*' All caps, italics, and three exclamation points."

I do remember Ken being rather relaxed when he called John and me to the set for blocking. We decided I would call my mother from Jim's desk, so my back would be to the door and I wouldn't see John enter. We discussed the kiss. We all agreed it should be simple, mutually savored, but not too elaborate. No tongue required. (Yes, we got that specific.) We rehearsed the blocking but never rehearsed the kiss. Then, the director sent us back to our trailers, with strict instructions that we were not to see each other until the scene began.

We were separated for at least an hour while they set the camera in a hidden location on the set. Because our characters didn't know this moment was being filmed, Ken didn't want us to see the cameras. He wanted everything to feel as real as possible.

After what felt like a lifetime, I was finally called to shoot. The set was dimly lit. I couldn't see any people or any cameras; it felt completely real. Ken quietly walked me over to Jim's desk. He told me that he didn't want to yell "action," because it might take me out of the reality of the scene. Instead, he told me, after he walked away, I should wait a few moments, and then start the scene. He assured me the cameras would be rolling.

When he walked away, I felt completely transported into a new reality. I was Pam, I was talking with my mother, and my heart was

John Krasinski, my partner in crime

breaking. I spoke into the phone, telling her I was in love with Jim, but I couldn't confess my feelings to him. Suddenly, Jim walked in the door. I turned and saw him and my heart felt like it might burst out of my chest. I wanted so much to tell him how I felt, but before I could, he kissed me. It was perfect.

The director yelled "cut." The producers came onstage from their hiding places and had that confident, satisfied look about them. Not to sound too braggy, but we all knew we'd done it. We'd just filmed one of the best first kisses ever on television. We did two more takes for safety. And that was that. It felt amazing. If only they all went this smoothly.

My next big onscreen kiss was for the movie *Blades of Glory*, a comedic kissing scene with Jon Heder. Unlike *The Office*, there was no month-long planning session. On the day of the shoot, we had a rehearsal and discussed the scene with the co-directors. They thought it would be funny if we "really go for it" during the kiss, since our characters had been so reserved for most of the film. Jon and I thought we understood what they meant by "really go for it."

Later that day, we shot the scene. Jon and I, remembering the note to "really go for it," did an over-the-top, passionate stage kiss, opening and closing our mouths and smashing them

> "It's easier to do an action scene than a love scene. I love fighting. When the camera's not rolling, I'll usually punch some of the actors just for fun."
> —Jessica Chastain

together. We did a few takes like this, but kept getting the same note: "That was really good guys, but when the kiss comes we need you to *really* go for it. Like, *really*, really go for it." We really wanted to get it right. So, on each additional take, Jon and I kissed harder and longer, our lips working overtime. But the directors still weren't happy.

Finally, after the fourth take, one of the directors came up to us and said, "Guys, there is no easy way to say this. We need you to use your tongues. We're in a close up and we can tell you're faking it. That's what we mean when we say 'go for it.' Tongues. Not length." Jon and I started laughing so hard. We'd totally misunderstood the note. The next take we "went for it," tongues and all. It was actually the first time either of us had used our tongue in a kissing scene. And it worked!

Speaking of tongue, I used plenty of it in my love scenes with John C. Reilly in *Walk Hard* (I just realized I've kissed a lot of Johns). Not only did we have a scene where I licked his face, we also filmed what is probably the most intimate love scene I've had to shoot so far. It was a highly choreographed, over-the-top, comedic sex scene, with lots of slapping, choking, grunting, face licking, and very little clothing. It was part love scene, part stunt.

At one point, I had to knee John in the groin, while he pretended to choke me. We practiced the blocking over and over again. Everyone knew what to expect, and when to expect it. It was almost like a dance. Even though it was a satirical comedy, when it came time to shoot the scene, John C. Reilly and I were nearly naked in bed together. I was wearing a nude thong and a strapless nude band over my breasts. John was totally naked except for a flesh-colored pouch that he wore over his penis. The purpose of these "outfits" was so that no nudity was accidentally caught on camera. But, in real life, they certainly didn't leave much to the imagination.

Our director, Jake Kasdan, was very respectful. He requested a "closed set." That meant no visitors, no photos, all video monitors showing the scene were to be shut off (except for his), and only crew members that were vital to the shooting of the scene were allowed on the set. Just so you know, this is something you can request should you ever be asked to film a love scene. Tell the director you want a "closed set" and they will give it you.

John and I were brought to set wearing robes, which we kept on until the very last second. As soon as Jake yelled "cut," the robes were rushed back to us, so that we didn't have to stand around nearly naked while getting notes and resetting for the next take. By the time the scene was over, we were exhausted and dripping in sweat. John C. Reilly and I bonded quickly that day. We had to trust one another, on a basic level. He's a very gifted actor, very committed to his craft, and

John C. Reilly and me from Walk Hard

I feel privileged to have worked with him. At the end of the movie, he gave me his penis pouch as a wrap gift.

I'm very lucky that I've never had a situation in which I felt compromised while shooting a love scene. I've always felt very safe and respected. An actress friend told me that a very well-known actor once put his hand up her skirt during a love scene. Mind you, this was not a planned move. She called over the director and said loudly, "I don't remember discussing him putting his hand up my skirt. Did I miss something in the rehearsal?" The director looked at the actor sternly and said, "No, we didn't discuss that. Don't do it again." Good director.

When it comes to love scenes and stunts, ultimately, *you* are in charge of your safety and comfort. If there is something you don't understand, ask. If there is something that makes you uncomfortable, speak up.

HOW TO BE A GOOD GUEST

It's not easy to come onto a working set, only to spend one or two days doing a small role. I've been there. It's kind of like being the only stranger at Thanksgiving. The regular actors will most likely be polite but not overly friendly. You won't get a lot of reassurance from the director; she will be more focused on the regular cast than on you. Your wardrobe will likely be rushed and ill-fitting. You won't have a friend to keep you company. It can be kind of a lonely experience. Despite these disadvantages, your job is to show up, lay low, do your work, and leave.

Imagine you've got a clogged toilet and you call a plumber to fix the problem. There is nothing more annoying than a plumber who arrives late, chats your ear off, slows you down, and tries to sell you a new bathtub. Don't be the actor version of that annoying plumber. Show up on time and prepared. Keep to yourself, and don't ask to take photos with the cast or invite the cast/director/producer to your upcoming improv show. Don't suggest additional dialogue or ways your character could return in later episodes. Don't worry about networking or standing out. Don't ask people about retrieving a copy of your work for your reel—your agent can call the production later and ask on your behalf. Just fix the toilet. Everyone will love you if you just show up and fix the toilet.

When I was on *That '70s Show*, I played Stacy Wanamaker, a snooty bridal store clerk who gives Jackie, played by Mila Kunis, a hard time. I was in two scenes with Mila Kunis and Wilmer Valderrama. It was the seventh season and also Topher Grace's last year on the show.

Now, I always get nervous when I start a new job. I can't help but worry about being good, and I also wonder how I'll fit in socially on set. I feel kind of like a little kid starting a new school. So, being the guest on a hit show amplified everything. The cast and crew were all friends; they had been doing the show for seven years together. I felt like a fifth wheel. No one talked to me during rehearsals. No one talked to me during breaks. No one asked me to have lunch. In fact, no one asked me a single question about myself. The only person who said more than "hello" and "goodbye" to me was Kurtwood Smith, who played the dad on the show. We chatted briefly at the snack table one day. I'm pretty sure no one learned my name. It felt so odd to me at the time, but I came to learn that this was very normal behavior. It doesn't make any of them jerks. In fact, I can't say enough good things about this group of people. They were talented, gracious, and very well liked. At the end of every tape night, the entire cast would go into the audience and sign autographs.

Imagine my surprise when Topher Grace stopped me as I was walking back to my dressing room after tape night. We hadn't been in any scenes together, so we were never formally introduced. He said "Hi, I'm Topher. You're Jenna? You played Stacy?" I said, "Yeah, that's me." He said, "Man, you were fantastic. You have this great, deadpan comic timing. I loved what you did in that scene. Really cool. How's

Me, as Stacy Wanamaker, on That '70s Show

it going for you?" I said, "Well, this was a big deal for me just now. But, it's been hard, you know? I'm struggling to get any job I can." He said, "Just keep doing what you are doing. People didn't totally get my thing at first either. But, you are really funny. Trust it. Great job." I blushed, and we shook hands and went our separate ways. But, *wow!* What a cool moment! Years later, when I was on *The Office*, we ran into one another at an awards party. He said, "I remember you! You were on *That '70s Show* and played the snooty shop owner. I knew you were gonna blow up one day. Congrats on everything!" Again, *wow!* Since then, Topher and I have become friends. We've starred in a movie together (*The Giant Mechanical Man*) and are even producing an animated television show together (*Adult Content*).

An actor going out of his way to be supportive is a rare thing. Like I said, most of the time you will leave the set wondering if anyone knew you had been there. Here's what I learned from Topher that day: Taking the time to say one, brief nice thing to a guest actor goes a long way. I've never forgotten this gesture, and I do my best to pay it forward. If you're nice to an aspiring actor, they will never forget you. I remember every single actor who took a moment to be generous with me when I was just starting out. Here they are: Molly Shannon, Topher Grace, John C. Reilly, Michael Douglas, Linda Cardellini, Robert Forster, the late Peter Boyle, and Matthew Lillard. They have my undying gratitude and loyalty.

My greatest example of a generous acting partner is Chris Messina, who worked with me in the movie *The Giant Mechanical Man*. Chris has worked with Woody Allen, Sam Mendes, Amy Adams, Jennifer Aniston, and many more. He is a great partner. He makes it his goal to give his partner whatever they need for their performance to be great.

One night while working on *The Giant Mechanical Man*, Chris and I had an outdoor scene on a train platform. We were shooting in Detroit, in the wintertime, and it was freezing. Chris played a street performer and was supposed to remain perfectly still, like a statue, while I delivered a long monologue. What's more, he was painted silver and standing on stilts. Meanwhile, my character was bundled up in a parka and wool cap. First, we did the wide shot. Then, when we moved in for my close up, I told Chris he could stand down and get warm. He didn't have any lines in the scene, and I didn't want him to freeze if he wasn't on camera. I was perfectly happy to look at a mark on a tall ladder, to help me pretend I was talking to him. Chris would hear none of this. He said he would absolutely stand there, no matter how long it took, because he believed it made a difference. Through multiple takes, he stood there, off camera, freezing in 10-degree weather. And he was right—it made a huge difference.

Unfortunately, not everyone is Chris Messina. I've worked with actors who didn't know their lines, actors who only cared about their side of a close up, and an actor who showed up to work with a debilitating hangover. I once attended a table read for a project during which the lead actor was sending emails on his smartphone from under the table. Another time I was doing a scene with an actor who forgot one of his lines and then loudly blamed *me*, saying, "I couldn't remember what I was supposed to say because of how she was looking at me." He was clearly embarrassed that he messed up, but instead of taking responsibility, he lashed out. I have a friend who did a play with an actor who for the first week of rehearsals refused to say any lines. He just barked at her like a dog. True story.

    I once worked with an actress who couldn't remember her lines. When it was time for my close up, she was messing up her dialogue so badly, it completely tanked my performance. During a break, the director suggested we do a take without her and have one of the production assistants read her lines off camera. I agreed, and he told the actress we were breaking for lunch. Then, when she left, he had me do two more takes without her. I was lucky the director advocated for me. You too might find yourself in a situation where you have to find creative ways to protect your performance, despite an unhelpful partner. This can be difficult when you're just starting out because you may not have the status to fight for what you need.

With Chris Messina on the set of The Giant Mechanical Man

Most actors I've worked with are kind, professional, and prepared, but every once in a while you get an unprofessional jerk. It doesn't happen too often, but if you find yourself in one of those situations, just remind yourself that the good news about acting jobs is that most of them don't last too long. If it's a few days on a project, or a few months, you can get through it. That said, if you are in a situation in which you feel you are being abused or harassed, tell someone. You shouldn't have to work in a situation like that, even for one day.

Shifting gears, let's talk a little bit about the actor's Code of Silence. Creative environments require people to expose themselves in very vulnerable ways. It's an intimate business we work in, without much privacy. But actors should be able to go to work and not have to worry about exposing themselves to the public. I've worked with a lot of big stars and heard about their private lives. Sometimes this was intentional; sometimes it was unintentional. But no matter what, I never repeated any of it. When I did *That '70s Show*, Wilmer Valderrama was in the midst of a tabloid-heavy relationship with Lindsay Lohan. Ashton Kutcher was with Demi Moore. While we were on set, I observed and overheard a lot of details about those relationships. I never told a soul. Not even my closest friends. I inherently felt that part of the job of a guest actor is to help maintain an environment for artists to feel safe being themselves.

Once I had a job with a very high-profile actress who kept leaving the makeup trailer to vomit. It happened three times. I knew she must be pregnant, and a few months later it was announced that I was right. I never told anyone. As for myself, one day I had to sign my divorce papers on the set of *The Office*. A clerk brought them to work, and I had to sign them in front of the cast and crew during a break in

> "My agent says that I'm a 'repeat business guy.' If you hire me to come do a movie, I'll be on time, know all my material, be ready to go, have a good attitude. I'm here to work, so I get hired over and over again by the same producers. If you just be a team player on set you can work so much more often."
>
> —Dean Cain

shooting. Another time I broke down crying on set when I got a message that my grandmother had died. I wept on the assistant director's shoulder. Everyone kept it to themselves.

So, if you're feeling gossipy, pretend you're a priest or a therapist and keep set banter confidential. Hopefully, one day you'll be the celebrity actor and need to count on other people's discretion. Don't spread gossip. And don't sell stories. Protect the artists. You're on the inside now, so be a member of the family.

EDDIE MURPHY AND WILL FERRELL

I was at a party once and heard a story about Eddie Murphy, told by a guy who'd played an extra in one of his movies. He told us that, at the beginning of the shoot, the extras were rounded up and sternly told, "Under no circumstances are you to speak to Mr. Murphy. In fact, don't look Mr. Murphy in the eye when he's on set." The actor telling the story implied that Eddie Murphy was a big jerk for having a rule like that. "Who does he think he is? We're all people! If I was famous, I would never do that. We're an artistic community!" Now, first of all, who knows if this guy was telling the truth? Who knows if Eddie Murphy has this rule or if it was just some PA trying to look important in front of the extras by giving them a bunch of rules? But, for argument's sake, let's pretend it's true, and Eddie Murphy demands people not speak to him or look him in the eye on set. Hold that thought while I tell you another story.

I've worked with Will Ferrell a few times, most notably on the movie *Blades of Glory*. This was a huge-budget movie and Will was the lead. He had a big job with lots of dialogue, elaborate costumes, and ice skating stunts. Here is what I observed: From the moment Will walked out of his trailer until the moment the director called "action," someone was speaking to him. "Hey, Will, how's it going? Can I get you anything? Do you need a coffee, Will? Water, Will? Anything, Will?

How was your weekend, Will? Cowbell, Will! Hey, Will, my son is a huge fan and tomorrow is his birthday; do you mind taping a little message for him? Hey, Will, when are you gonna host *SNL* again? What team you rooting for this weekend, Will?" It was crazy. Every step the man took, someone was talking to him. He couldn't even take a breath. Now, Will is pretty much the nicest man in the world. He seemed to speak to everyone. But I couldn't help but wonder how he is able to concentrate. Somehow, he can. The attention seems to work for him. Or, at least, it doesn't rattle him. Could you imagine if, on your way into an audition, every single person you encountered from your car to the casting office was speaking to you or staring at you or taking your photo? Could you give a good performance? Not me. It's unnerving and distracting. I'm a nervous and shy person. I feel vulnerable when I have to perform. I need space to focus. Will seems like a naturally social person. He must somehow thrive on the energy of connecting with people. That's not me. Luckily, I'm not faced with this problem. People don't talk to me all day or ask for photos. But, if that did start happening to me, I'd probably need to create some boundaries to do my job well.

Which brings us back to Eddie Murphy. If his process requires him to be left alone, I'm not one to judge. The pressure and attention is so great for a lead actor. Millions of dollars are being gambled on his (or her) ability to deliver a great performance. Eddie has done a number of movies where he portrays multiple characters, which means he's got to remember improvisations he did as the dad character that need responses when he's dressed like the mom. For Pete's sake, if the man needs space, give him space. And don't judge him for it.

As long as the actor's need is communicated with kindness, a request like this should be met with respect. I believe it is our job to nurture and protect one another. You wouldn't judge an Olympic athlete who doesn't want to chat you up moments before hitting the uneven bars. Resist the temptation to become cynical, judgmental, and negative about your fellow artists.

Most importantly, don't be judgmental about what *you* need to thrive as an artist, either. The more you work, the more you will learn a process that helps you give the best performance possible, which includes everything from your preparation time to your time on set. What routines can you adopt to center yourself? I did a play in New York and I had to share a dressing room with the other actors. I found myself having a hard time focusing right before the show. I brought some headphones and listened to a thirty-minute playlist while I put on my makeup each night. I couldn't worry about the other actors thinking I was antisocial. I had to walk out onstage and give a performance. For me, the time to chat was after the performance.

Don't be afraid to be a little self-indulgent. It's okay to have rituals. It's okay to have needs. The important thing is that we find a way to create a mutually satisfying environment.

If you ever need a quick reference guide for on-set etiquette, keep the list on the next page handy. Dog-ear it, review it, follow it—and you'll contribute to the creative, constructive experience that your fellow actors, the crew, and the director are looking for.

The Do's and Don'ts On Set

Do

Read every script you receive, and check for new changes

Be honest with Wardrobe about your sizes

Be on time

Check in with a Production Assistant when you arrive

Bring your ID and Social Security card or passport

Bring specialty food items and snacks if needed

Know your lines

Be prepared to wait—a lot

Eat the free food

Help to create a safe environment for everyone

Ask questions if you don't understand something

Find out what you need to thrive

Don't

Take or post photos of the actors, the set, or yourself at work

Post information/spoilers about the job on social media

Ask for professional favors from the cast or director

Gossip

Allow another actor or director to take advantage of you

Stop a scene in the middle (just keep going until you hear "cut")

Judge your fellow actors

Take things personally

CHAPTER SIX
THE JOURNEY

"Perseverance is not a long race; it is many short races one after another."
—WALTER ELLIOT

I had been living in Los Angeles for two years, when one day I walked into a Pottery Barn and suddenly suffered an anxiety attack. I had gone to Pottery Barn to buy a friend something off her bridal registry and panicked when I couldn't afford a single item on her list. As I looked around the store, I wondered if I would ever be able to afford to shop in a place like this.

My friend was twenty-four, had a good job, and was getting married. Her list included all sorts of adult things like a handcrafted dinnerware set and 400-thread count sheets. My life was a complete mess. I was living with a stranger I'd found through a roommate matching company after my first roommate gave up acting and moved back home. My credit card had gone into default. My acting career was nonexistent. I *still* wasn't in the union and hadn't heard from my agent in months. Oh, and I'd almost just accidentally become a high-priced call girl. My future looked like an endless tunnel of rejection and shitty apartments filled with thrift store crap.

So, I lost it. Right there in Pottery Barn, sitting on one of their beautiful Chesterfield leather sofas that I couldn't afford, I lost my shit. *What the hell am I doing?* I thought. *No one cares that I'm here.* Between sobs, I heard cheerful Christmas music playing in the store. Oh my God. I couldn't take another extended family Christmas party with questions like "When am I going to see you on TV?" and "How's Holly*weird* treating you?" I seriously wanted to quit.

I often tell this story when I speak to acting students. Because of all the questions I get, aspiring actors mostly want to know how to endure the rejection, confusion, doubts, and seemingly insurmountable hurdles of an acting career. I wish there was an easy answer. All I can say is, "I've been there." Every artist has a different journey, and you'll have to figure out yours—you'll have to determine how much you can endure. Because the roadblocks, doubts, and insecurity are all part of living an artistic life.

> "The difference between successful people and others is how long they spend feeling sorry for themselves."
> —Barbara Corcoran

Back there in Pottery Barn, to keep going, I had to adjust my expectations about what it meant to be an actor. First, I needed to accept that things weren't going to happen quickly. A lot of my anxiety was coming from my belief that I was failing because things were "taking so long." I needed to stop comparing myself to other people and commit to an actor's life, with all its ups and downs. Then, I needed to change my approach. Being an actor is a lifestyle. I wasn't able to shop at Pottery Barn because I hadn't chosen the well-worn path of a conventional job. I had chosen the path of an artist. I needed to embrace my decision.

The Journey

If I could go back and give sobbing Jenna some advice to make it easier, here's what I would say:

Step One: Give yourself permission to be an actor. Don't apologize for being weird. Live an unashamed artistic life.
Step Two: Create your own work.
Step Three: Never give up.

Ultimately, you have to find your own way. And you will. So be patient with yourself. Try to embrace the journey. And, maybe try to stay out of Pottery Barn until you book your first big job.

MY PATH

Most of my struggling years were spent trying to stay busy enough that I wouldn't notice that the phone wasn't ringing. I did things like create a detailed card catalog of all the casting directors for whom I had auditioned. I wrote down what I wore, how I felt I did, and if I got a callback. This card catalog served no practical purpose. It was 100 percent something I did to keep from going mad. I stopped updating it years ago, but I still have it sitting on a shelf in my office.

> ZANE, BONNIE
> 1999 Tested for NIKKI pilot
> 11/19 AUDITION - Untitled Detective Pilot - ABC
> (wore Santa Barbara jeans, blue multi shirt, brown boots)
> CALL-BACK + test!
> 1/7 AUDITION - Untitled 30s Project - Pilot - ABC
> David Ronn, Jay Sherick - writ/producers
> (wore plaid skirt, black sleeveless top - straight/curly hair)
> 1/29 AUDITION - Dexter Prep by Paul Simms
> on tape
> 3/7 Producers pilot - 2006 role of Jessica
> black top, jeans + boots

When I worked short temp jobs as a receptionist, I would sometimes speak in different accents. Yes, that's a little weird, especially when you consider that I'm horrible at accents. But I didn't care. Sometimes I'd go people watching, or sit at a diner and eavesdrop on conversations. I liked studying the way people behaved in different situations. I especially liked listening to people fight. I guess that's the ambulance chaser in me. Guess what: When people get really, really mad, they often get quieter, not louder. Cool thing to try in my next fight scene. In between my various auditions for *The Office,* which happened over the course of a few months, I did everyday tasks while pretending to be Pam. I grocery shopped, did laundry, and went to the movies as Pam. Pam is a person who has a hard time standing up for herself. So, for example, when someone cut in front of me at the grocery store, I said nothing. As Jenna, I would have spoken up. But as Pam, I just stewed silently. I created so many details about Pam's life that it became easy to improvise at my auditions. (I still do this exercise sometimes when preparing for a new role.)

Another project I did to keep myself occupied was to develop and perform a Silent Comedic Magic Show. Yep, you read that right: Silent, Comedic, Magic. Here's how it all began: I was at a party and my friend Brian started doing funny fake magic tricks using his hands and fingers. It was something he'd been doing for years as a party gag. It was hilarious. After I begged him, he gave me permission to develop it into an act. I went home and worked on it, eventually perfecting five "tricks." Then I made a series of homemade props, bought a second-hand tuxedo, slicked my hair back, and got myself booked in comedy clubs. (I so wish I had a photo of myself doing this.)

> "Careers are a jungle gym, not a ladder."
> —Sheryl Sandberg

At the small comedy clubs, to get on the docket you had to bring your own audience. The more people you brought, the better your time slot. So, I did my act a handful of times, inviting everyone I knew. It was always fun, and people always laughed. I loved performing it. Until one night, at a place in the Valley, I didn't have a single person show up. Zero guests. The booker took pity on me and said I could do my act anyway. He put me up second to last. When my turn came, as I walked to the stage in my vintage tuxedo, carrying my various accessories, I heard someone mumble under their breath, "Oh, great, prop comedy." It felt like a punch in the gut. I did my best to ignore him and went on stage anyway. I performed my first trick and no one laughed. Nothing. Oof. This was a tough room, and I had four more tricks to go. For the second trick, I held up a sign asking for a volunteer from the audience. No one raised their hand. I just stood there in silence, holding a piece of poster board. Crickets. Oh my God. My five-minute act suddenly felt three hours long. I was so humiliated. I skipped that trick and quickly got through the final three, then slumped off the stage to sympathy applause. That was the last time I ever did my comedy magic act. Talk about going out with a whimper.

But, seriously, I loved that act. I love that I did it. It didn't get me discovered by any agents or casting directors, nor did it get me auditions or offers from producers. But it got me out of the house. It gave me a place to focus all of my unused creative energy. I was going to comedy clubs, watching other people perform, and surrounding myself with creative people. That act kept me going for about seven months. It fed my soul. Until that night in the Valley when it crushed it.

After the magic act was shelved, I needed a new outlet. I started drawing. Even though I had never drawn anything in my life, I decided to try drawing my own autobiographical comic book. I enrolled in a drawing class at my local Learning Center and bought a dozen books on how to draw comics. I started by drawing

> "I would credit my woodworking as an entirely separate creative outlet, refreshingly unconnected to the show biz. I used to love nothing more than driving away from some sweaty test audition for a pilot, heading to my shop and making something, anything, out of wood. The satisfaction of tangibly creating something tactile that I could hold and see and enjoy, on which no network or studio could give me notes, was priceless."
>
> —Nick Offerman

one panel a day. A friend saw my drawings and asked me to collaborate with her on a book to help people with eye strain. So, I illustrated a book on eye strain (never published), which then lead to my illustrating a coloring book for a man who ran a center for children with hearing disabilities.

It felt good to produce something. It felt good to have no one but myself to please. My drawing was a safe way to escape the pains of rejection and longing during my years of waiting for a break.

As a matter of fact, if you are looking for an escape right now, you might consider coloring the following sketch of Old King Cole on the next page. Yep, that's right, made by me during my struggling actor days. Enjoy!

Doing my silent comedy act and learning to draw were nice distractions, but I found the most fulfilling activity was when I volunteered for an animal charity as a foster parent. It was my job to house, care for, and rehabilitate sick and injured cats or kittens, and then find them a forever home. If you're looking to quickly escape from your self-obsessed, self-involved actor brain, try nursing a litter of sickly five-week-old kittens back to health. Nothing made me forget about losing a job faster than trying to wrangle eye drops into the goopy faces of flea-ridden cats fresh from the pound, or waking up every few hours to feed them around the clock. Over the course of three years, I fostered and found homes for fourteen cats. I can't tell you how much I needed this kind of selfless volunteer work. Having an obligation to something bigger than my own ambition made my life feel more meaningful. And, oh my God, the kittens were so cute!

During this time, I remember being at a particularly horrible audition with a particularly nasty casting director. It was a situation that, in the past, would have left me in a puddle of my own tears for days. But instead, after she condescended to me, I thought, *Screw you, lady. Yesterday I drove two hours and fished a box of abandoned kittens out of a filthy dumpster. You can take your shitty two-line role and shove it.*

King Cole

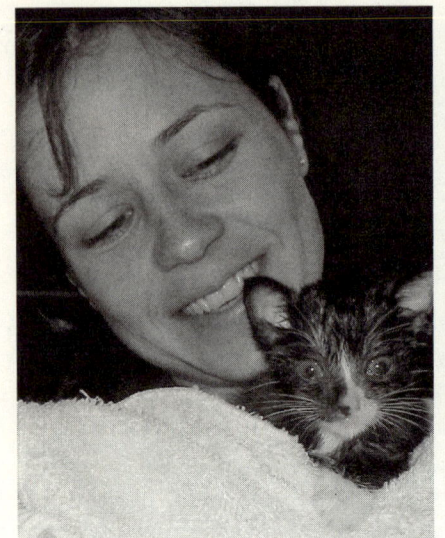

Two of my foster kittens, Katie and Ellie

Having that box of kittens put things in perspective. My entire self-worth wasn't riding on an audition. Ironically, as a result, I started doing better. My auditions were better because I didn't *need* it all so much. And you can't fake that. You can't fake not needing it. Ever notice how you do so much better at the auditions you don't really care about? When I started doing the rescue work, I felt a calling that was separate from acting. It made all of my auditions less important to me. And that seemed to make people more interested. Funny how that works.

I didn't come to these life-changing ideas all by myself. I was lucky enough to find a book called *The Artist's Way* by Julia Cameron. *The Artist's Way* is a twelve-week, self-led creativity seminar in the form of a book. Almost every aspiring actor I know eventually finds *The Artist's Way*. But while many people start the book, few actually finish. It took me two tries. It's challenging. Each week you read a new chapter and confront the obstacles that are blocking you from moving forward as an artist. The greatest thing about the book is that it's active. It's a workbook. You aren't just reading about *how* to be creative; you are actually *being* creative, writing and performing and finding new ways to express yourself. In my case, it was *The Artist's Way* that got me to create my magic show and start drawing. And, by the end of the twelve weeks, I had written a treatment for a movie that I later filmed with my friends. If you ever find yourself uncontrollably sobbing in a Pottery Barn (or Crate and Barrel), go buy *The Artist's Way*.

> "Other actors are not my concern, and that's their life and that's their journey. Everybody has to get to a point in their own time and their own way."
> —Zachary Quinto

TAKE RISKS

I soldiered on and, after three more years in Los Angeles, finally found myself with an agent and a manager. I was in SAG. I was getting auditions. I was a member of a terrific theater company and had learned great audition techniques. But more importantly, I was getting callbacks and had even booked a few small roles. Things were starting to feel legit. A few years after the Pottery Barn fiasco, I finally felt like I'd figured out what it meant to be an actor.

But I was still earning the bulk of my money from my day job as a receptionist. And while I was booking small acting jobs here and there, I couldn't seem to break out of the Bit Player Club. My characters rarely had a name. I played "College Girl #1" or "Waitress." The point of my roles was usually to relay plot information, such as "Yes, I saw the suspect around midnight. She was covered in blood." Or to set up the main actor for a big comedic moment, like "I have a delivery for Mr. Thompson. One blow-up doll?" I was working my ass off to get five minutes on your TV a few times a year.

I had figured out the essentials of the business, but now I had a new dilemma: I was stuck. I didn't want jobs—I wanted a career. I wanted to earn my living as an actor. No more day job, no more catering on the side. I wanted to play characters with real names and juicy plots. How did people do that?

I reminded myself that I was the CEO of my acting business. If it wasn't moving in the direction I wanted, it was my responsibility to make it happen. Rather than sit around complaining, I needed to take action. I decided to look at my "company" with a more critical eye and ask, "Where can I make improvements?"

I landed on my agent, Charlie. I loved Charlie on a personal level. I trusted him. He'd been a great champion of mine, which is worth a lot. On the other hand, Charlie was at a smaller agency with only three agents. And while Charlie and I had a great relationship, the head of the agency never took a shine to me. Around this time the third agent, a woman I really liked, left to start a management business of her own. So now I was at an agency with only two agents, and one of them didn't even like me. While Charlie could get me auditions for smaller one-day roles on television shows, he was having a harder time getting me in the door for the bigger stuff. And the fact that the head of the agency was unenthusiastic about me meant that she wouldn't be putting her muscle and resources behind me. My manager, Naomi, was getting me meetings with people like Judd Apatow and huge casting directors like Bonnie Zane and Allison Jones. And those meetings were leading to big things like testing for my first pilot. I wanted my whole team to be as effective as Naomi. If I looked at the situation strategically, rather than emotionally, it was clear that it was time for me to find a new agent.

> "Life shrinks or expands in proportion to one's courage."
> —Anaïs Nin

Naomi was very excited when I told her I was ready to make a change. She had wanted me to move for a while, but any time she even tried to discuss changing agents, I'd dig in and refuse to budge. Part of my stubbornness was out of loyalty. But if I'm being honest, the bigger part was out of fear. What if I couldn't book the bigger roles? At least now I could blame my agent. But if I had access to more prestigious auditions, I'd only have myself to blame if my career didn't take off. Basically, it was easier to complain about the career I didn't have than to take action and make it happen. I have known a lot of actors who've stayed with the wrong agent because they believed it's better to have any agent than no agent at all, or because they're afraid to take risks, do the work, be rejected, or have hurt feelings. But staying in a situation that doesn't serve you is a career killer.

Over the years Charlie would joke with me, "Jenna, one day you're going to leave me for the big time." And I'd always say, "I hope so, Charlie. I hope so." And we would chuckle. But when the time came to tell him I was ready to move on, I was anything but laughing. Charlie was kind. He said he was disappointed but also that he understood. He told me he loves the challenge of building a new career, and he knows that, if he does his job well, people will outgrow him. There was hugging, tears, and well-wishing.

Naomi and I spoke about what new agent might be best for me. Her top pick was an agent we'll call "Tom." Tom was the head of a medium-sized agency, tenacious, and well respected for having a good eye for talent. Naomi had another actress client with Tom who was constantly going out for lead roles in pilots and big guest star roles, and her résumé was not much bigger than mine.

Thanks to Naomi's connection, Tom looked at my reel and agreed to meet with me. Luckily, we clicked. Our first pilot season together, I had more auditions than I could have ever imagined. I also started booking lead guest roles. It was during our time together that I booked my big guest role on *That '70s Show*, a recurring role on *Six Feet Under*, and the pilot for *Rubbing Charlie*. We were a good team.

Two years later, I was earning as much money from my acting work as I had as a full-time administrative assistant. After seven years in Los Angeles, I was finally able to quit my day job. Clearly, changing agents was a risk that paid off. But as fruitful as our relationship was, Tom wasn't my last agent. After *The Office* became a big hit, I moved on to William Morris Endeavor (WME), where I am today. At the bigger agencies you get a team of specialists. They assign you a different agent for every area of the business. It's something the medium-sized agencies just can't do. So now I have a bunch of agents: two for film, one for television, one for theater, two for publishing, one for voiceover work, and one for advertising/commercials. They have the ability to package films and television shows or to even help me develop my own projects.

Here's the bottom line: You are in charge of your momentum. If you are feeling stalled or experiencing a "drought," you must try anything and everything to reset the course of your career. Ask yourself if there's a risk you aren't taking. Is there a move you should make? Maybe it's not a professional move but a personal one, like ditching a roommate that weighs you down. Or getting out of a day job that has completely derailed your focus. Maybe get out of town; go camping; sign up for a yoga retreat. How long since you took an acting class?

> "Courage doesn't always roar. Sometimes courage is the quiet voice at the end of the day saying, 'I will try again tomorrow.'"
> —Mary Anne Radmacher

I have a friend who got a job at a coffee shop as a barista because the owner promised him flexible hours and plenty of time to pursue his acting career. Two years later he was the manager. He was so busy with the coffee shop that he had to put his acting career on hold. When I asked him why he didn't quit, he said he "felt bad because the owner was going through an ugly divorce and needed him to keep the shop going while she figured things out." It was the type of thing that could go on forever. I asked him, "Did you really move all the way to Los Angeles to run a coffee shop? You could have done that at home." It was the wake-up call he needed. He gave his notice and now works very happily as an actor and theater producer.

CREATE YOUR OWN WORK

I know I've said it before, but it's worth repeating here: The single best thing an actor can do, both professionally and personally, is to create their own work. This could be as simple as memorizing a Shakespearean monologue and performing it in Washington Square Park. Or maybe start a podcast with a friend. Or write a play. Or start your own YouTube channel. Whatever you do, I promise it will create momentum.

Take, for example, the time then-struggling actor Rob McElhenney approached his actor friends Charlie Day and Glenn Howerton about an idea for a TV show. Rob recently explained his inspiration: "It was just an idea of a guy going over to another guy's house to ask him for sugar, and the other guy telling him that he has cancer. And instead of the friend being compassionate, he just wants to get the sugar and get out the door. I knew that nobody else would think that was funny except Glenn and Charlie. So I wrote a script and showed it to them."

Using their own camera, they shot a pilot episode for less than $200. They showed the pilot to various studios, and it was picked up by FX for a full season. The show, *It's Always Sunny in Philadelphia*, was just renewed for both a twelfth and thirteenth season in 2016.

One of my favorite examples of the benefits that can come from creating your own work is my friend Mark Proksch, who had a recurring role as Dwight's handyman for two seasons on *The Office*. If you aren't familiar with Mark, go to YouTube and search "K-Strass Yo Yo Guy." You won't be sorry. K-Strass is a character that Mark created, a self-proclaimed yo-yo master who's actually terrible at the yo-yo. In a series of hilarious pranks, Mark got K-Strass booked as a guest on various local news programs in the Midwest. The result is absurdly hilarious. When the writers of *The Office* discovered his videos, they offered him a recurring role on the show.

Here's Mark's amazing story, in his own words:

I was living in Milwaukee (2010) working at a small content marketing firm. I had been in and out of grad school, taking temp jobs when needed, basically doing my best at avoiding any sort of career. I had been working on short films with a group of friends and took those around the festival circuit, but nothing really came of it. I was always acting in the films and doing silly characters that I found funny. Then my friend Joe Pickett and I came up with the idea of booking one of my characters, Kenny "K-Strass" Strasser, a self-destructing, self-proclaimed yo-yo master, onto local morning news shows.

The morning of my first appearance I woke up at 4 AM. I needed to drive two hours from Milwaukee to Green Bay. It was winter and I remember lying in bed thinking that the last thing I wanted to do was get out of my warm bed and drive to Green Bay in the middle of a blizzard. But then I thought, what the hell else am I doing?

After the first couple morning show appearances, people started uploading them to YouTube. I was bummed at first because I figured it would blow my cover and I wouldn't be able to do any more appearances. This turned out to be true. What I didn't even fathom was that people out in Los Angeles were becoming fans.

Not in my wildest imagination did I think goofing around on morning shows to make my friends laugh would lead to a career in Hollywood. But I think that's why it worked so well: I was just doing something I loved to do without the worry of expectations.

Mark has been working in Los Angeles as an actor and writer ever since. Oh, he also ended up marrying Amelie Gillete, the writer from *The Office* who first discovered him. He got a wife *and* a career out of making his own work. That's an amazing story, right?!

I also experienced a major breakthrough as a result of creating my own work. Inspired by Rob Reiner's masterpiece *This Is Spinal Tap*, I had an idea for a "mockumentary" based on a group of misguided charity workers. Not being a writer, I didn't have a script, so I invited some actor friends over one Saturday afternoon. I set up a camera, explained my idea, and asked everyone to improvise. Over the next few hours we pretended we were holding our first meeting for a very special charity. We had a blast. We did this exercise a few more times and, eventually, I transcribed the tapes and wrote a script. It was far from perfect. Still, I thought, *Let's shoot this thing for real. It will still be improvised, but now we have an outline that we can use as a blueprint.*

I set out to make our movie look as "real" as possible. I thought, *What if we could trick people into thinking this was a real documentary about these dreadful people?* So, we purposely made the camera-work messy and the actors were allowed to regard the camera if they wanted. We even filmed talking head interviews with each character.

Over the course of a year we shot our little movie on the weekends or whenever everyone was available. When it was finished, we got into a few short film festivals. It seemed like the whole thing was going to be another Silent Comedic Magic Show—fun times but ultimately leading nowhere. But shortly after I finished the project, I was called in to audition for the American version of *The Office*. I couldn't believe my luck. I'd just spent the last year of my life practicing the mock-documentary style of acting, and here I was being asked to audition for a television show that was conceived in the same style. I have no doubt this experience played in my favor as I auditioned.

Another important milestone that came from my self-made movie: It was the first project I'd actually finished. Over the years I'd started many creative projects but failed to finish a single one of them. Once I finished my movie, I knew I could finish anything. And, I have. Here's the trick I used to help me get through: Whatever you decide to make, tell yourself it's going to suck. Want to write a script? Good! It's going to be awful. Want to film a web series with your friends? Fantastic! It's going to be dreadful. Whatever you do, know that it's going to be a disgusting mess of awfulness. And then, *do it anyway*. Something awful is better than something incomplete. Because the only way to improve is to finish something, look at it, learn from it, and then start something new. The new thing will be better. And then the thing after that, and the thing after that. But you can't get better if you don't finish anything. My movie isn't great. It is clunky and choppy and has bad sound. But it's also funny and daring and weird, and I love it. And now I'm a finisher. I finish things.

> "Done is better than perfect."
> —Sheryl Sandberg

Every project you finish has value. Whether it's the one-woman show you wrote, the web series with only twenty-four views, the pilot you wrote with your friend, all are important and will pay off somehow. Putting things in the vault is important. I have a friend who has been writing a hilarious and irreverent series of children's books for the past two years. She's a struggling actress who said to me one day, "I don't know why I keep doing these books. No one is going to publish them. At the very least they keep me sane and I love them." And I said to her, "One day you're going to break out in a big way. I just know it. And your new fancy agent is going to ask you what ideas you have. You will go into your vault, pull out this series of children's books, and say that you have a fully developed idea for an animated series. And it will happen." Because that's how this stuff works. When you become a busy working actor you won't have time to fill the vault. So, fill it now! A successful writer I've known for years has a stack of at least a dozen scripts she wrote during her years as a struggling writer. They are all great. Now that she is a success, she can dust them off, give them a polish, and get them produced. To the outsider it looks as if she's writing three genius scripts a year. Nope. She has her vault.

I JUST GOT FIRED

Oh my God. This is very humbling. I just got fired.

Ouch.

Let me take a moment to collect my thoughts...

Wow. This sucks.

And it's also a bit embarrassing. I mean, here I am writing the chapter of my book that's all about the struggle and how it never really ends, and an artist's life has many ups and downs, and you have to learn to stay positive and embrace the journey . . . blah blah blah . . . I just got fired.

Let me back up.

After a lovely break from acting, where I had a second child and stayed home to be a momma, I decided it was time to go back to work. So, I did a pilot for CBS starring Matt LeBlanc about a dad who has to take on more parenting responsibilities when his wife (me) goes back to work. It was a multi-camera sitcom, filmed at a studio fifteen minutes from my house, with family-friendly hours that allowed me to drop my son off at school every morning and be home for dinner each night. Not only that, but it was directed by legendary sitcom director James Burrows (*Friends, Will & Grace, Mike & Molly* . . . basically every great three-camera comedy you've ever seen), and created by a writing team from *That '70s Show*, Jeff and Jackie Filgo. Great cast, great paycheck, family-friendly. *I'm the luckiest gal in the world,* I thought. I enter back into the workforce and land a great gig right out of the gate.

So, we shot the pilot and it felt great. Everyone loved everyone. The audience laughed; the network seemed happy. Hugs and kisses all around. We were clearly destined for a pick-up. "See ya soon!" we all said as we left the stages on our last day of work. No one said words like "hopefully" or "fingers crossed." I mean, come on: CBS, Matt LeBlanc, Jenna Fischer, James Burrows, Jeff and Jackie Filgo—we were getting picked up for sure. One month later, the day all of the pilots were getting news of their pick-ups, my phone rings. On the line are all of my agents, my manager, and my publicist. I thought, *They must be calling to congratulate me on my new television series!*

"It's bad news," they started out.

"What?! We didn't get picked up? That's crazy! That makes no sense! Everyone said it was a sure thing!"

Silence on the line.

"No, it's worse than that, Jenna."

"What do you mean? Oh, no . . . Did I get . . . fired?"

"Yes. Focus groups didn't like the chemistry between you and Matt. They just didn't believe you as a couple. So, the network is moving ahead with the show but letting you go, since it's Matt's show. We're really sorry."

Oof. Kick in the stomach. I went from having the perfect job to having no job.

I immediately went to a dark place. I figured it must be me. It must be that I sucked, that I was horrible. I told my agents I wanted to see the pilot. I wanted to see my performance, in case there was anything I could learn from the experience for next time. Thankfully, CBS agreed to send me a link. My husband and I watched it, and you know what? We loved my performance. I was upbeat and funny and charming. I thought I did a great job. But, I have to admit that Matt and I, despite getting along very well off-camera, seemed mismatched as husband and wife. Somehow it didn't make sense. Chemistry is a tricky thing. It probably didn't help that we were both so well known for other roles. I learned later that a common comment in the focus groups was, "I just don't believe Pam would marry Joey." Ugh.

Dealing with It

Even though I'm happy with my performance, it's not making the rejection any easier. So how am I dealing with it? Eating a corn dog. And Oreos. And ice cream. Potato chips. Gucamole. While writing this paragraph, I ate a half bag of Doritos. As it turns out, not only is food the best part of getting an acting job, it's also the best part of being fired. (By the way, early in our discussion of this book, my publisher suggested I write advice about what to do if you get fired, as it's a pretty common thing in this business. I told him it was a great idea, but I couldn't give that advice because I'd never been fired. Well, now I've been fired. I hope you're happy, Glenn.)

To everyone on the outside, I seem to be taking the news "very well." But on the inside I feel heavy and hopeless. I'm doing weird things like waking up extra early to do my hair and makeup and wear high heels to drop my son off at school in the morning. "Look at me, everyone! I'm not totally freaking out and feeling worthless. You can tell by my beautiful hair and shoes!" Then, I'll come home and crawl in bed. (Except I can't really crawl into bed because I have this book to write, floors to sweep, and my daughter's birthday party to plan.)

I've toyed with the idea of getting bangs. I sent the following photo to all of my friends, and they all told me not to do it.

I've started Googling stories of other actors who have been fired. It turns out, Glenn was right—this really does happen a lot. And everyone seems to survive. In fact, I discovered that three other actors have been fired from James Burrows' shows and all of them have gone on to do great things. They are Lisa Kudrow (fired from *Frasier*), Ray Romano (fired from *NewsRadio*), and Bob Odenkirk (fired from *Will & Grace*). I'm thinking of getting the four of us together for a show called *Canned by Burrows*. I think it could be a hit. (But I'll probably get recast.)

I found an amazing transcript of a 2010 commencement speech that Lisa Kudrow gave about her experience of being fired. It lifted me up. The link is at the bottom of this page in case you need it one day.[1]

I also started reaching out to my actor friends, telling them I had been fired. It turns out almost all of them had been fired at some point in their careers, too. I told them my story; they told me theirs. It felt so good to know I wasn't alone. I started feeling like I might be okay. This is why that family of artists I told you to find in chapter one is so very important. They are the only people who will really understand at a time like this. Your parents will try to understand. Your best friend from college, who works for a nonprofit, will kind of understand. But your artist friends will completely get it. And they will know exactly what to say when you reach out for help. Take, for example, this amazing email I got from my friend Sean Gunn when I wrote and asked him the question, "Any thoughts on being fired and how to deal with the deep pit of self-doubt and despair it brings?"

> "Success is the ability to go from failure to failure without losing your enthusiasm."
> —Winston Churchill

He responded: "Yes. I had a conversation many years ago about getting fired with some friends, saying we knew it would happen sooner or later. We made a pact that when it did, we would go out and celebrate. Since then, we have done just that, and it's quite liberating. So crack open a nice bottle you've been saving for a special occasion, or maybe get a sitter and go out on the town, and enjoy. You deserve it."

So, on the day CBS was set to publicly announce the news of my firing, I took Sean's advice and celebrated. We hired a sitter, my husband took me to Palm Springs, I got drunk, and I went swimming. I created this photo essay:

---

[1] http://www.graduationwisdom.com/speeches/0075-kudrow.htm

"How to Deal with Being Fired"
By: Jenna Fischer

Man, that felt good!

And that pretty much brings us to today. I've been in Los Angeles for twenty years, and I'm still looking at the phone, wondering if any exciting jobs will come my way. Such is the actor's life. At one point, I considered calling this book *The Actor's Life: Struggle, Work, Repeat*. But perhaps a more accurate title would be *The Actor's Life: Struggle, Struggle, Struggle, Cry, Think-You-Should-Give-Up, Work, Repeat*.

You see, here is the truth I've learned after twenty years in the business: No job really changes everything. Nothing removes the struggle completely. When I look back over my career, there are so many moments that I thought would "change everything." Pilots I tested for that didn't happen, pilots I got that were never picked up, a recurring role on *Six Feet Under* that I was positive would change everything, films that didn't go anywhere. In many ways, *The Office* did "change everything." Doors open more easily for me, I get offered roles, and I have a nice savings account. But I still go to auditions. I still get rejected. And I still get fired. Even after an Emmy nomination and ten years on an award-winning television show, I'm still fighting it out for the next thing.

I've also learned that the jobs you don't get often make way for better opportunities in the future. And that has certainly been the case for me. Shortly after getting fired from the Matt LeBlanc show, I was offered the leading role in a new Steve Martin play, *Meteor Shower*. The play was an amazing experience. I spent an entire summer rehearsing and collaborating with Steve Martin, one of my idols. I grew so much as an artist, much more than I would have playing the exasperated wife on a weekly sitcom—I'm sure of it.

When the play was finished, I was offered a job playing Ben Stiller's wife in the film *Brad's Status* written and directed by Mike White, two more of my idols. I even starred in an episode of one of my favorite television shows, *Drunk History*. None of these opportunities would have been possible if I'd still had my job on the sitcom. Crazy how it works, right? While I was drowning my sorrows

Josh Stamberg, me, Steve Martin, Alexandra Henrikson, Greg Germann

in Palm Springs, I had no idea that the void would be filled with such wonderful new opportunities.

    So, after such a crazy, unpredictable year, I find myself returning to the question I posed back in chapter one: *Why do I want to be an actor?* The truth is, I don't have one definitive answer to this question. Because over the years my answers have changed, or been added to, so that now I find I have a wide variety. Of course, the simple answer is because I love it. Even with all the ups and downs, I love being an actor. But more specifically, I love using my imagination. I love reflecting on my own feelings and bringing them to life in a character. I love connecting with an audience. I love being in touch with how it feels to be guilty, angry, regretful, elated, loved, loving, spiteful, terrified, dishonest, or heroic. I love to recreate and experience these feelings onstage, on TV, or in film. I love figuring out a character, discovering how we're similar and how we differ. I love all the new challenges that come with a new project. I love being a storyteller. I love making people laugh. I love being with and creating with other artists. And I love celebrating the human experience.

Over the years, I've received letters from people telling me that watching *The Office* helped ease the pain of their cancer treatments, or that watching one of my movies made them laugh for the first time after the death of a loved one. I can't tell you how moved I am to be a part of something that means so much to people. Because I've experienced this myself. In 2007, while attending a work event in New York City, I fell down a flight of stairs and fractured four bones in my back. It was awful and very painful; I couldn't leave my bed for more than three weeks. My manager Naomi sent over the complete box set of *The Larry Sanders Show*. Oh my God. I'll never forget watching those episodes, because as soon as the opening credits started to play, the pain in my back disappeared. It was better than painkillers. The great Garry Shandling and all of the people who made that show were just trying to make people laugh. But they ended up doing so much more for me. They say, "Laughter is the best medicine." It is a truly humbling experience to think I've been part of the medicine for someone else.

As I was putting together this book, I went through boxes and boxes of old photographs. I came across one from May 1996, taken outside our house in St. Louis. It's me, my mom, my dad, and our dog, Lizzie. One of the striking things about the photo is that only my mom and Lizzie are looking at the camera; my dad and I are looking down. My sister took the photo, and she must have been calling to Lizzie to look at the camera, which is probably why my dad and I are preoccupied with the dog. So funny, this kind of photograph doesn't happen anymore. Nowadays, if someone isn't looking at the camera, we can check instantly and keep snapping until we get it right. The other unfortunate thing I notice about this photo is my clothes. If at the time, someone told me that this photograph would go into a book I'd write twenty years later, I probably would have worn a different outfit.

But the most important detail about this photo, the reason it's in this book, is that it was taken moments before I was to get in my car and drive the eighteen hundred miles to Los Angeles. If I could go back and talk to that girl, there is so much advice I'd give to her, starting with the sandals. I'd also probably say something sensible about expectations, telling her that it's going to be a long journey, baby steps of progress, and to not lose hope. And most of all, I'd tell her I'm proud of her, that it takes guts to embrace your life so emphatically and chase your dreams.

But since I can't say that to her, I'm saying it to you. I'm proud of you for taking this leap. You've chosen an unpredictable life, but certainly a life worth living. Go forward, embrace the journey head-on, with all of its ups and downs. More than at any time in recent memory, we are in need of artists and stories to remind us of our shared humanity. As you go forward, though you may get discouraged, please don't hold back your gift. Because the world needs actors. The world needs you.

Now, go do it.

ACTOR INTERVIEWS
SHARING THE BRUSHSTROKES

Matt Weiner, the creator of *Mad Men*, wrote an article for aspiring artists in which he said this:

> *Artists frequently hide the steps that lead to their masterpieces. They want their work and their career to be shrouded in the mystery that it all came out at once. It's called hiding the brushstrokes, and those who do it are doing a disservice to people who admire their work and seek to emulate them. If you don't get to see the notes, the rewrites, and the steps, it's easy to look at a finished product and be under the illusion that it just came pouring out of someone's head like that. People who are young, or still struggling, can get easily discouraged, because they can't do it like they thought it was done. An artwork is a finished product, and it should be, but I always swore to myself that I would not hide my brushstrokes.*

The truth is: Being an artist is hard. Writing is hard. Acting is hard. Directing is hard. Making music is hard. I know your relatives at home think, *How hard can it be? It's just playing pretend*, but it's hard. Most of the time it will feel like you are pushing a boulder up a mountain. But if you keep going, the muscle that moves you forward will get stronger. You learn to press on even when you don't want to.

All too often we compare ourselves to the results we see in other artists without the knowledge of the full journey it took to achieve those results. With the idea of "sharing our brushstrokes" in mind, I asked four actor friends of mine to share their journey with you.

NATALIE ZEA

Natalie Zea on the set of The Detour

My friend Natalie Zea is a successful television actress. Like me, she is happy to be on the small screen, developing and playing a character over a long period of time. Unlike me, Natalie started earning her living as an actress fairly quickly after leaving school. She's done national commercials and voiceover campaigns; she was the star of a soap opera; and she has had both regular and recurring roles on such shows as *Dirty Sexy Money*, *Hung*, *Californication*, *The Following*, *Justified*, and *The Detour*. She also does movies. And Shakespeare. She does comedy. She does drama. She does it all. Wait, did I tell you that she's tall, beautiful, funny, effortlessly stylish, and easy to work with?

With all of these advantages, I always assumed things came easily for her. But as I learned when we sat down for a chat, she's had to battle it out, job to job, like the rest of us. Hers is the story of a consistently working actor, with all its ups and downs.

So, I have to start at the beginning: When did you decide that you wanted to be an actress?
I didn't really think about it seriously until I was a freshman in high school. My cousin was in the drama club and she insisted that I join. I was kind of quiet in the back of the class, until one day we were doing auditions for a student film, a really intense, emotional scene. It was a scene where a gunman was holding me hostage—and I just went there, sobbing and everything. Afterward I thought, "I could do this forever." So I guess it was then. Freshman year of high school.

Did you want to go to college or pursue acting right out of high school?
No, I wanted to be really legit. I wanted to go to Juilliard. I also knew I needed to be in New York. And I needed to live the dream.

New York was the dream, not LA?
LA or the "Hollywood" thing was never the dream. It was always, always New York. I wanted to wait tables and live in a dingy basement apartment. My high school drama teacher played such a huge part in getting me to where I wanted to be. She kind of brainwashed me. She taught me, when people asked where I wanted to be in ten years, to respond by saying, "I want to be a working actor." I didn't even really know what that meant. It was just a thing to say. But yeah, when I started out, I just wanted to be working.

Did you audition for Juilliard?
I did and I got as far as the callback level—which was actually a big victory for me. But, ultimately, I didn't get in. For a long time, I felt

like I would never be a part of the "A" squad because I wasn't a Juilliard graduate. But I would have been in school two years longer if I was in that program. Who knows what my career trajectory would have been? I'm also not sure it would have properly prepared me for a career in TV, so I'm finally okay with it.

You ended up at American Musical and Dramatic Academy on a scholarship. Did you like your school?
I did. But, I quit after the first year because I felt like—I was being a little brat—I felt like they were selling a bill of goods. But, really, I just didn't feel like I was the "star." So, I quit and thought, "Okay, I'm going to do this on my own." I didn't even know the first thing about how to get a headshot. It was a good lesson for me because later, I had to eat some humble pie, and I wrote them a letter saying "I've made a mistake. I don't know what I'm doing. I would be honored if you could take me back." And they took me back—they said, "We are revoking your scholarship, but will take you back." And I was like, okay.

Besides acting technique, what is the most valuable thing you learned from school?
There was an acting class that met three days a week and it was really long, like four hours or something crazy, and one of the professors—he was one of the reasons I quit initially; he ended up being one of my favorites, of course—he had a zero-tolerance policy about tardiness. If you were late, you got shut out. And if you missed a certain amount of classes, you got kicked out of school. So it was a domino effect. So, now, I'm never late. And if I am, it's extenuating circumstances and people get phone calls and apologies.

So you get out of school, you are nice and poor, and what happens?
I booked the first two things I auditioned for! One was a short film, and the producer on the short film had a friend who was an agent at

Paradigm. And he said, "I think you should meet with him." He auditioned me and signed me. He ended up being my first agent.

Even though you had the personal recommendation of the producer friend, you still had to audition for the agent?
Yeah, and I ate a carrot in my audition scene. I thought I would stand out by eating a carrot. There was no carrot in the scene. It was so weird. Don't do it. Strong but wrong. But they signed me and I thought, "Oh, this is gonna happen." The second thing I booked, before they signed me, was the short film that led to the feature film *Boys Don't Cry*. I played Chloë Sevigny's part. We workshopped it—we basically wrote that movie. It was supposed to be a feature but we ran out of money. We ended up shooting about a third of it, and they cobbled that together and made it a short and, later, Kim Pierce was able to make it into a feature. The sad thing is that I never got to see the short. I've still never seen it. But those were the first two things I auditioned for and booked, so I thought, "Piece of cake, man."

Which was great until the next two years happen and I can't get arrested. I was auditioning my face off. I was auditioning for the best shit. Big movies. Pilots. Everything. Commercials. And I just couldn't book a thing.

What changed?
After like two years I finally book a Snickers commercial. I couldn't be more excited. I really need the money and I finally have a professional credit. From there things very slowly pick up. I do a few more commercials and I end up getting a TV guest-star credit a year later and somehow—I don't know how this happened to this day—I got a pretty great voiceover campaign out of nowhere and from there I started doing voiceovers. Then, I ended up getting a play—not through my agent but on my own. *Measure for Measure*. I was finally able to quit bartending because I was making enough money with voiceovers and

commercials, and this was a really great period for me. I was unencumbered; I was a working actor.

A working actor just two years out of school! I'm so jealous!
But then, the commercial strike happened. And it was like, fuck, this was the only way I'm making money right now. I could live on savings for a little while, but I'm going have to figure something out.

Is this when you booked the soap opera *Passions*?
Well, let me back up. Earlier that year, I flew to LA with my writing partner—we were both actresses at the time, and we decided we were going to do one pilot season in LA to see how it went. Because in New York it just wasn't the same. So we rented a place with another friend of mine who was there permanently and she killed it. I mean she went out on everything, tested a million times. She didn't book anything but she tested a million times and was just the talk of the town. And I just wasn't quite there. But at the very end of that pilot season there was this new soap opera they were casting called *Passions*. I was like, "Yes, I will do anything." And the writing was horrible. It was like really, really, really bad but, whatever, it's a job. I auditioned and tested but didn't get the role.

So, I flew back to New York and that's when I got all the voiceover work. I was in that really great play and then the strike hit. I'm trying to figure out what to do because I'm running out of money and out of nowhere, I get a call saying, "*Passions* wants to audition you again."

The new role was Amanda. Amanda was a cousin of somebody. So I tested. It was fine, whatever; I wasn't invested. I got back to New York, got the call, "You didn't get it." A week later I get a call that they want me to come out and test *again* for Amanda. My first response was "Did you throw the tape away? Because I'm not going to do anything different. And if you didn't want me, you didn't want me."

Were they paying for you to fly back and forth all these times?
Ha! Yes. That's a big reason why I kept going back. I figured, whatever, I'm not going to do anything differently in the test but I really miss my friends in LA so in my mind it was just a social trip. So I went; I tested again. I got back to my hotel and my agent calls to tell me I got the job. But it wasn't for Amanda. It was to replace the girl who got the role I'd originally auditioned for because she hated it and wanted to leave. And, I cried—not tears of joy. I wasn't all that happy. But, you know, you sign contracts. So I was like, I guess I'm moving to LA.

And now you are taking over this role, which must have been weird.
Exactly. Yeah. Plus, we didn't look anything alike. Nothing alike. Different hair color. Everything. Very weird. I show up to set and they just didn't know what they were doing with me. They put me in these pantsuits and the weird helmet hair and the bad brown lip liner that made my lips look somehow thinner and weird-colored eyeshadow. Everything was wrong and bad. I easily looked twenty years older than I was. But I didn't know that I could say, "Hey, let's not do this. Let's do something that makes me look good." Which is a huge lesson to learn. You don't have to just accept what they do to you. You can say it in the nicest way that it isn't working for you.

So I looked crazy and old and weird and I hated the character. The dialogue was awful. Around this time, I had a big falling out with my group of friends that lived here. So not only was I living here doing a job that I hated, but I'm totally lonely. I'm basically just waiting out my contract. I liked having the money but I couldn't do it for more than two years. So I saved really well. I was always really hyper-aware. I mean I did do things I was never able to do before, like shop at Barney's, but like shop at the warehouse sale. A lot of people on the show were scared or had gotten comfortable and used to the security. One of the actresses thought I was crazy and said, "Do you know what it's like out there?" And I said, "Yes! Of course I know what it's like. It's awful. But it's worse here."

Time passes, the two years are up. You're free. And now you are in Los Angeles. Back to the grind, I guess.
Yes, and immediately after leaving *Passions*, I booked the very first guest star that I auditioned for. It was a tiny little role on a show that was, I don't even remember the name of it but Peter Horton was directing and he and I became fast friends. So again, I'm thinking, "This is going to be a piece of cake." And then I didn't book anything again for a year.

Nothing? For a whole year?
Not one thing.

That's rough. What broke the drought?
The Shield. Peter Horton was also directing an episode of *The Shield* that I auditioned for and he was like, "You, I love you, of course." It was a guest spot that ended up recurring.

It's funny because I think of you as a person who's always been working, but you have actually had many droughts you've had to fight to get through. You've spent a lot of time working, but you also spent a lot of time looking for work.
Yeah, nothing is being handed to me. There was a third drought too. That was the one where I thought, "I don't know if I can do this anymore." That was a huge one.

When was that?
It was right after my very first series regular role for a show called *Eyes*. I booked it and I thought, "This is it. I'm done. Sign me up on

my new house and all my new cars and my jet. This is my big break. This is going to be huge and I don't have to worry anymore." And we got cancelled after five episodes. We shot thirteen but we got pulled very unceremoniously. No phone call or anything. It was a great show too. That was the biggest blow that I think I've ever felt. So, I had a real breakdown. I just couldn't crawl out of that hole because I had set myself up way too big. That was the one where I thought I might need to hang it up and look for something else to do.

What did you do?
After a gin-infused, poor-decision-making afternoon, I lost my mind and went to Paris for six weeks. And Paris really did it for me. I had such a miserable time there, that after I got back I felt invigorated and ready to conquer. I just needed an attitude adjustment really and within a couple months, maybe less, maybe like six weeks, I ended up getting the series *Dirty Sexy Money*. Since then, it's been pretty steady. But that was the hardest.

Since then, anytime anything I've done that has fallen through or not been picked up or whatever, I've been okay. Because that blow, that *Eyes* blow was so hard. I said I was never going get my heart broken like that again. I'm able to keep a little distance from it all now.

That's very interesting. I had a big "I'm quitting" moment too. Right after the first pilot I did—this crazy show starring Scott Wolf that didn't get picked up. I really had to fight my way back from that low. I feel like, at some point, everybody has their "I'm leaving this business" moment. And then you either leave the business or find the will to press on and something changes. I developed a callus, not in a bad way, but I developed a callus after that. You kind of have to. For example, I got fired from a very high-profile job recently, and it did not crush me as much as my Scott Wolf pilot not going.

Exactly! There have been things way worse than that *Eyes* thing not happening but shit happens. You have to get your first heartbreak out of the way and after that you realize everything's going to be fine. Even if it's not, it's still going to be fine.

Have you ever had something totally crazy happen to you on set that pulled your focus? I don't know if people realize how much craziness there is to absorb—changes to the script, wardrobe stuff, changes to the schedule—that you have to block out in order to stay focused on the work. Yes, I did this guest spot on a network show once—I tend to shy away from network stuff partially because of what I'm about to tell you. They just have lots of rules and shit. There is way more freedom and independence in cable. Anyway, in *Under the Dome*, I was playing a very powerful, sort of strong, evil villainess and there was a scene where I had to straddle this guy, fully clothed, while delivering a monologue. I do the fitting and we find this incredible outfit. It's a long, tight, leather pencil skirt, total designer duds—very cool. The wardrobe people say, "The script says you have to straddle him, which you can't do in this outfit." And I'm like, "Let's show them a picture of the outfit and if they love it we'll just work around it." So, we do. And we are told they love the outfit. Great.

I get on set, dressed in the skirt, ready to start rehearsal and the director says, "You are supposed to straddle him in this scene." I kind of laugh and say, "Well, obviously, we can't do that in this skirt. My legs don't really ... the skirt is so tight ... can we block it another way? Maybe I'm standing over him?" Crickets. So I say, "Ummmm ... okay, if you're really tied to the straddle thing then we should just put me in some pants. No problem. Happy to change." Crickets. He says, "Let's see you do the straddle with this on." I'm like, "Well it's just not really physically possible." But he insists, "Well can we see you do it?" Okay. So, I pull my skirt up to my waist and straddle the other actor and I say, "Is this what you want?" The director says, "Well obviously, no."

Then, they call the wardrobe people in, and the script supervisor is there and they get the writer on the phone and it's suddenly a huge national thing. I'm like, *what the fuck is going on right now?* So I say, "It's so simple, guys. We need to do one of two things. We're either going to change the outfit or we're going to change the blocking. That's it." They say, "Go back to your trailer, we have to figure this out." So, I'm in my trailer and I hear the PA outside talking to someone on their headset saying, "Yeah, I don't know how long we will be, the actress doesn't want to do the blocking so we're going to have to figure something out."

Oh, I hate that.
So I open the door and say, "Excuse me, excuse me, I don't know who you're talking to but that's not the case here." The director comes into my trailer, closes the door, sits down and says, "We're going to have to figure this out." So I say, again, "It's so easy, you put me in pants or you change the blocking. I can't say it any more times. I don't know how to say it any differently." This went on for an hour. I ended up wearing the skirt and side-straddling him or something.

Why couldn't you just put on some pants?
I don't know. 'Cause the network really liked the skirt but they wouldn't change the script.

When this happens, does this get in your head? Oh no, I'm getting labeled as "difficult" even though I'm acting totally rationally?
Yes, of course.

What do you do with that anxiety?
Well you just have to throw it away. Any reasonable person can see that this is outrageous and I'm not being difficult. I honestly did feel like I was being gaslighted. I don't know how anyone else could have

handled it differently. Although, if I'd been a series regular, with that kind of status, there would not have been a discussion. I could have said, "No, I'm wearing jeans." "Oh but we wanted—" "I'm wearing jeans. The end. We do not have time to have this ridiculous discussion." But I didn't. I was a guest star.

That's an amazing story. I feel so validated for my million stories I have like that. Thank you.
We all have them.

You recently went back and gave a commencement speech to the graduating students of your acting school. You had some amazing advice. Do you mind sharing some here?
First of all, a little background, at the end of each year they would have an agent come and speak to the graduates. They sort of tell you the ins and outs of the business, talk about how tough it is out there. Then, the agent scouts a student that he thinks is going make it and that student gets a private phone call. So I like to start by telling the students, "I just want you to know I didn't get that phone call. So it doesn't mean shit. And if you did, great. But if you're one of the ones, like me, who didn't get the phone call, it doesn't mean shit."

And also, that acting is a noble profession. We are told "no" all the time. Sometimes several times a day, over and over again and we keep doing it. I think there's a lot of nobility in that. Don't let people tell you that it's superficial or not hard work or that there's no emotional fallout or psychic fallout from it, because there is. Which is why I stress being kind to each other as artists. It's really easy to be sitting in waiting rooms thinking of each other as the enemy, but the further along you get in your career, the more you're going to realize that the people who stuck it out are actually really good people and they're your allies.

And finally, I thought that being an artist meant being all consumed by my art and not being able to have a full, rich life outside of it, and the more successful I became the more I learned that that's not how it goes. In order to be able to portray people in the real world, you have to have experiences in the real world. That was something that I couldn't conceptualize when I was starting out. I would just eat, breathe, think, love acting. After a while it's just boring.

Is there anything you would tell young Natalie? If you could go back?
Yes. That it's not going to happen right away and it's not going to happen the way you think it's going to happen, but it's going to be great. Just stick with it.

SEAN GUNN

Rehearsals for Guardians of the Galaxy *with Zoe Saldana, Chris Pratt, director James Gunn, Dave Bautista, and Sean Gunn*

I grew up five minutes away from Sean in the suburbs of St. Louis, Missouri. At the age of six he enrolled in a summer school acting class taught by my mother, Anne. I remember my mom telling his mom that he was "born to be an actor." He was one of the youngest and smallest kids in the class but my mom cast him as the narrator of the play because he was the only one who could read all of the dialogue, and because the narrator had to be funny and dramatic and engage the audience. At just six years old, Sean could do it all. In high school, he acted in the plays and musicals at my all-girls school. Despite attending different schools, we stayed in touch over those many years.

When we both settled in Los Angeles, we became real friends. Sean has always been a big supporter of my acting. He suggested me for two roles that created career-altering opportunities for me. One was for a small role in a pilot presentation that led to me meeting my now manager Naomi Odenkirk. The other was for a staged reading of a movie that led to my first speaking role in a film. Sean is an example of a person who loves the craft of acting. He doesn't chase fame or money or status. If anything, he chases skill. He's curious and thoughtful and his main ambition is to live an actor's life. He was the first of my friends to get in the union, the first to get an agent, the first to land a national commercial, and the first to land a regular job on a TV show. Success came easily for Sean early on. And then, it didn't. He suffered a long drought of ten years in which he had to work harder than he did when he first arrived. And now, he's one of the stars of the *Guardians of the Galaxy* franchise.

Sean, ever since I've known you, you've wanted to be an actor.
Yeah, I'm one of those annoying actors who never wanted to do anything else. From the time I was old enough to know what a profession was, I told anyone who would listen that I was going to be an actor. It got to the point where, even though I was a smart kid, I didn't try as hard as I could have in high school because I told my parents that I was going to an acting conservatory where my grades wouldn't matter so much.

Ha! So what happened after high school?
I auditioned for the four best acting conservatories in the country—according to one person's list, at least—and gained acceptance at one: The Theatre School at DePaul University (aka The

Goodman School of Drama). I packed my bags and moved from St. Louis to the big city of Chicago.

How was it?
Great! It was all-inclusive. All acting and performance classes all the time: scene study, voice and speech, movement, makeup, stage combat, everything. It was a weird place for a lot of reasons, but I was kind of a weird dude and I really felt at home there in a way I never had in high school. I loved learning about acting and theater. The problem was, The Goodman had one of those cutthroat programs where they cut people after each of the first two years. Or actually you had to be "asked to return," which was their way of getting around using the word "cut."

That sounds terrifying.
It was pretty intense for an eighteen-year-old kid who wasn't finished growing yet physically, and probably hadn't even started growing emotionally. I recently heard that The Goodman doesn't "ask students back" anymore. I remarked that was probably a good thing, but my good friend Michael Rooker, another alum, said, "Hell no! That was the best preparation I had for how tough and filled with rejection it would be on the outside!" I see both sides. But I learned later from one of my teachers that I had come perilously close to being cut, and I think it would have devastated me in a way that I can't imagine. To this day I have enormous respect for the students who were cut and stuck with it, but there aren't many.

What do you feel like you gained from attending an all-inclusive acting conservatory like The Goodman?
There are three specific things I gained from acting school. The first was that I was able to get myself to a physically neutral state for my body type, to become more of a "blank canvas." When I started, my posture was atrocious. Through four years of movement classes,

yoga, and the like, and particularly through simple awareness of what my body was doing, I stood up straight and was able to relax into a neutral position, which made it easier to tackle any role. This is crucial for an actor.

I'm very jealous. I didn't have movement classes in school. It wasn't until very recently that I finally invested in a one-year movement and body course called Feldenkrais that I found that command of my body.
I studied Feldenkrais in school! The Goodman had an interdisciplinary philosophy that exposed us to various types of study, and I'm grateful for that. But what I'm probably most grateful for is the second thing I wanted to mention, and that's the friends and colleagues I made. People like Valentine Miele, Lee Kirk, Judy Greer, and John Cabrera are all friends I met in school and are people with whom I still collaborate today, and who provide the base of my community of actors (and writers, directors, producers). And they are all close friends, of course. Oftentimes I tell actors that the best thing they can do if they want to get started is to find other people whose work they admire and who they can spend their time with, trading ideas, and roll up their sleeves and tackle whatever projects are interesting them at the time. When I moved to LA, I already had those people.

That's huge. You had your tribe of artists when you moved. Huge.
Yes, they hadn't all come to Los Angeles yet, but they would in time. The third thing, tied to the second, was simply the ability to view myself as an actor. To have the confidence to embark on the profession and to have the proper respect and reverence for it that I think is helpful for any actor. To put it another way, rather than wanting to be an actor to avoid getting a "real" job, I learned that being an actor *is* a real job.

I'm curious, what made you decide to move to LA over, say, New York or to stay in Chicago? Because I remember that you were booking a number of jobs out of Chicago while you were living there.
I don't think I ever really considered moving to New York. For one thing, I'm a terrible singer, which cuts down the number of jobs I'm eligible for. And besides, I really wanted to make a living, and there are more paying jobs and more content created in LA.

It also seems like you were more interested in doing film and television than theater. Would you say that's true?
I love theater and I had directed a play in Chicago that I was very proud of, but when you added it all up, maybe a few hundred people saw it. Then I did a ridiculous commercial for the Illinois Lottery Commission and everyone I knew saw it. I was getting calls from aunts and uncles, cousins, old friends from elementary school. But it wasn't anything I was particularly proud of, other than the paycheck part—I was just out of school and quite the snob at that time. I wanted to marry these two ideas—there had to be a way to do work I thought was exciting and cool but that a lot of people saw. Then I shot a small independent movie in Wisconsin, cast out of Chicago, but that had a couple of LA actors as well. I got to be friends with a fine actor named Jamie Kennedy. We would go out to dinner at night, and when we returned to the hotel Jamie would have scripts that his agent had delivered for him to read and see if he was interested. This blew my mind. I thought, "I want *that*. I want scripts delivered to my door," and I made plans to move to LA immediately.

How was it after you first moved?
Jamie took me under his wing and gave me loads of helpful advice—he had been grinding for nearly a decade before his career took off and he knew the ropes. I had done just enough commercials in Chicago to keep me afloat so I never had to get a "day job." But I think the

one thing I wish I had known was how paltry my résumé looked to an LA casting director. I had done seven commercials and two independent movies in under a year and had graduated from one of the most prestigious acting schools in the country, which I thought was pretty impressive for a twenty-three-year-old. It wasn't.

So, how did you push ahead? How did you find your first agent/manager?
In my case it was pretty much blind luck. I met a manager who was an old acting teacher of my friend Lee Kirk (not sure if you've ever met him) [Lee is Jenna's husband]. It was a very good time to be my "type" in the late '90s—there were lots of roles for the quirky nerdy guys—and he signed me. I booked both of the first two TV auditions I went on. Finding an agent or manager in LA is almost impossible, because if you ask 100 actors how they found their first rep, you'll get 100 different stories. There's no road map; if there was, that's what everyone would do.

How did your expectations of what it meant to be an actor line up with reality once you started working? What were some of the most surprising differences?
It was quite jarring when I started working professionally and realized just how little rehearsal you get when you are working on camera. I think many actors who have extensive theater training feel that shock. Rehearsal is almost entirely replaced with personal preparation. The auditioning part is mostly the same, or quite similar, but once you land the job, that's it.

Have you ever done something that you considered to be a big risk and how did it play out?
I remember an audition I had for a recurring guest star on a Fox TV show that asked for a "Spicoli-type" (Sean Penn's character from *Fast Times at Ridgemont High*), that is, a surfer dude. Someone had just

been fired so they were under the gun, and they called in about twelve good comedic character guys, of which I was one. I looked around the room and saw all these guys doing their best gnarly surfer guy, and heard people through the door reading and I just didn't think the character was funny that way. So I took the lines written for a surfer guy and performed them like Leslie Nielsen on *Police Squad!* Totally deadpan. I remember the audition was at Fox so it took me a while to get to my car, and I booked the job before I exited the lot.

Before I congratulate myself too thoroughly for this victory (and it gets even better—I also had a callback for an NBC sitcom guest star earlier that same day and they booked me about an hour later. Little did I know on that twofer day that later I would have a drought of a full calendar year where I didn't book a job), I want to point out that I actually don't really think of this as a risk. When the consequence is "not getting the job," pretty much *nothing* you do is risky, because chances are you won't get it anyway. Every actor should remember that if it's not fun for you, it's not fun for the audience. So if you can't find a way in, change it.

How long after you moved to LA did you land your role on *Gilmore Girls*?
I moved to LA in late 1997, got my first agent in the spring of 1998, and did my first episode of *Gilmore Girls* in the fall of 2000.

Wow! Just three years. It took me three years just to get into the union. Now, if I remember correctly, the role on *Gilmore Girls* didn't start as a series regular. It went from a one-time guest spot to a recurring to a series regular role, right? It's the myth we all hear about when we are just starting out and it actually happened to you.
Yeah, my original role on *Gilmore* was a small co-star role as the "DSL Installer." I was supposed to work one day. I had one scene, about twelve lines or so. Amy (Sherman-Palladino, the creator of the show)

had a specific idea about pace and tone for the show. It reminded me of the old film comedies from Howard Hawks and Preston Sturges—movies like *Bringing Up Baby*, *His Girl Friday*, and *The Lady Eve*. It was all fast-paced dialogue and what I would call "precision timing" for how the jokes landed. I was a student and fan of those films and inherently grasped it without having to be told. I could tell from the writing what she was going for. I knew I needed to bring my best deadpan to the material. Like most great acting jobs, it took both luck and skill—the luck of finding a writer whose style I "got," and the skill to execute the job. So when Amy needed another actor for a walk-on role two episodes later, a delivery guy, she literally said to Jami Rudofsky, one of the casting directors, "get me a guy like the guy who played the DSL Installer." I will forever be indebted to Jami for replying, "Why don't I just get that same guy?" And it snowballed from there. I never thought I would end up on the show for so long. Amy was collecting quirky characters for her fictional town, and my deadpan-guy fit right in. They kept bringing me back and it eventually evolved into my character, Kirk. After two seasons they made me a series regular, and it lasted seven seasons. Even now, seventeen years later, I'm still playing the character. [In 2016, Netflix did a revival of *Gilmore Girls* and the series regulars reprised their roles for a special reunion season.]

What was it like when *Gilmore Girls* ended in 2007? I ask this because a lot of people assume that there is some "finish line" and once you've been a part of a hit show or big movie it's smooth sailing.
Even I assumed I'd have a lot more job opportunities come my way than I did. I had come off seven seasons on *Gilmore Girls*, a hit show, playing a very popular character. I had achieved a decent amount of relative success. I was fortunate enough to have a nice arc on another show (ABC's *October Road*) soon after, but it was cancelled and then I had years of crickets. I had thought I'd have my choice of projects,

but I actually had a harder time getting auditions than I had before I became a regular on *Gilmore Girls*. I think a lot of casting directors had literally forgotten who I was. I wandered around the acting desert before I realized I was even there. I had gotten less hungry, lazier, more complacent, and entitled.

What did you do?
I had to smack myself in the ass, go back to class, and pretend like I was starting over. It took me nearly a decade to achieve a level where I felt like I was successful again, and now I'm determined not to repeat my mistake.

Is there any part of being an actor that you struggle with more than others?
My biggest struggle is always that I'm not working enough. I love acting as much as I did when I was kid, and when I have droughts where I'm not doing it I start to go a little crazy. I would say 2016 was the first year of my career where my actual number of days acting on set was at a satisfying level.

So it only took you nineteen years to have a year that left you satisfied. That's good for people to know! How do you deal with the droughts?
Peace of mind in your personal life is an absolutely crucial element to your development as an actor. That's the biggest thing I've learned as I've gotten older. I have a lot of things that I'm interested in that keep me sane—cooking, writing, music, my cats, animal rescue, poker. Staying engaged with the world and other people more than anything.

But I also want to stress that staying in class is something I've found quite helpful. I think it's essential for every actor at least from time to time. It's more opportunity to do exactly the type of role I want to do at any moment, and it keeps me thinking like an actor.

If you could give three pieces of advice to a new actor what would they be?

First, act as much as you can. Get in class, do student films, put up a play. Any time someone asks you to act, say yes. And generate your own stuff too.

Second, and I said this earlier, find people whose work you admire, and whose work ethic you admire and surround yourself with them as much as you can. I'm not talking about stupid networking like trying to get in good artificially with people above you on the totem pole. I'm talking about other people at your level who might be struggling along with you. Build a community. You will all pull each other up eventually.

Third, stay curious about human beings and the human experience. Talk to people who *aren't* in the entertainment industry and listen to their story, ask them questions about what makes them tick. This can be much harder than you might think when you live in LA. Compassion for people, and a desire to understand them, will make your work better.

If you are driven by fame and success you are setting yourself up for failure. Even if you get it, you are unlikely to be happy, because unbridled ambition is a disease that only gets larger and eats more of you. It has to be about the work. Actors are storytellers, and we are students of the human condition. We do it because we love people, and we are trying to understand what it means to be one. That's the most important thing that I can express.

DEREK WATERS

Jason Ritter, Derek Waters, and me on the set of Drunk History

My friend Derek Waters created and appears on the Comedy Central television show *Drunk History*. He claims he created the show because no one else would give him an acting job. I have to say, this is not entirely true. Derek has appeared in numerous television shows and movies. What is true, however, is that Derek is definitely a creative force. He's created, pitched, and sold many television shows. He's financed and produced countless shorts. He's worked with heavy hitters like Will Ferrell, Sarah Silverman, Marc Maron, Bob Odenkirk, and Zooey Deschanel, just to name a few. (Seriously, the full list would last several pages.) He's well known and well respected in the comedy world.

Derek and I met while performing a pilot presentation called *The Pit* at the HBO Workspace way back in 2002. We share a manager, Naomi Odenkirk. We had the same acting coach, Robert D'Avanzo. We even have a few of the same film credits. But the thing that bonds us together is a love of creating. He's also just an all-around good guy. He's nice. He has integrity. He's been driving the same Toyota 4Runner he bought fourteen years ago with the money from his first big acting gig, because if Derek has extra money, he'd rather finance a new project than anything else. He's a great example of what can happen through making your own work.

Thank you for doing this.
I'm a little nervous because I haven't really made it as a working actor.

You don't think of yourself as having made it as a working actor? You're the creator of a successful television series . . .
That I act in. The only acting jobs I ever get are when I pick me. So that's my secret: If you want to work as an actor, hire yourself.

Well, that's not entirely true. We were in *Hall Pass* together. You didn't make that. I could probably name a dozen things. But let's start at the beginning. Did you go to school for acting?
Sort of. After I graduated high school, I went to community college—not to brag. I took a bunch of classes, but I ended up only sticking with acting and English, and left with a 4.0 after one semester. I moved to Toronto to study at The Second City. That was my college. At least that's what I told my parents. I was there for six months and then moved to LA when I was twenty.

When I got here, I remember I was at an audition, and in the waiting room were twelve girls and me, and we are all reading for the same role. So weird. I'm thinking, "Well, I hope they go another way with it." The casting director came out and said, "Summer Davis?" (I'm making up this name.) Nothing. No one gets up. The casting director keeps asking, "Summer Davis? Summer Davis?" Suddenly, the girl next to me said, "I'm sorry, did you say Summer Davis? Sorry, I changed my name yesterday. Yes, I'm here." I was like, did I really just get to witness that? That was amazing. I am definitely in LA now.

Why did you only stay at The Second City for six months?
I got kicked out of Toronto for being an illegal alien. I think you'll like this story. When I first got out here, I got really close to getting on *MAD TV*, so I was meeting with a lot of different managers. I told one of the managers about getting kicked out of Toronto and he goes, "Look, if you're with me, you gotta put jokes in your story. I'm gonna be setting you up with the head of Paramount, the head of New Line, you gotta put jokes in your story. So when you say you got kicked out of Toronto for being an illegal alien, say it like this: 'I got kicked out of Toronto for being an illegal alien. I mean, *me*. Can you believe *that*?'"

That was his example of putting jokes in your story?
Yeah. And I remember he sat me next to a loud fan which made it hard for me to hear his shit advice with his legs up on his desk. He ended the meeting by saying, "Derek, I love you but I've got the next Rosie O'Donnell on hold."

Did he end up becoming your manager?
No.

Did he not offer or did you not accept?
I didn't get *MAD TV*.

So him becoming your manager was contingent on you booking *MAD TV*?
Probably. But I'm glad it went the way it did. My first six to eight months here, I didn't know my shit yet. I needed to learn a lot before getting an agent or manager or being on TV. I needed to take classes and just meet people. So I started interning at Improv Olympic—which is a fancy way of saying cleaning toilets—so I could take classes for free. I was also performing at Second City and taking classes. I thought if I did all that, that good things would happen. I had a lot of faith in God and myself. I prayed a lot and just tried to be involved in things.

Did you have other day jobs?
I worked at Tower Records. I worked at a restaurant as a busboy. I would get little commercials every once in a while . . . I was somehow always able to get my green bean sandwich.

Green Bean Sandwich? That's real? What does that consist of?
You know, a can of green beans on a sandwich. A little butter. A little Old Bay Seasoning from Baltimore. Reminded me of home.

That sounds disgusting.
It was. But there was no other choice. That was my go-to when I was broke.

What moved you into the finer things like pizza and grilled cheese?
Commercials. I was performing at Second City and that's how I got my commercial agent. Booking my first commercial was the coolest thing in the world. It shot in Dallas, Texas. They flew me there. That was like, man, this feels so cool. I just got paid to act.

Oh, but here's a really terrible story, but a good story for this. After that, I got an audition for Axe deodorant. And in the "hilarious" commercial, the idea is that I'm coming home for my family reunion and right before the group picture's about to be taken, I get introduced to my second cousin. We shake hands and then she smells me, and my deodorant is so great and powerful, she throws me down, and starts trying to kiss me. I'm supposed to be, like, resisting and pushing her off me. But, yep. That's the commercial. Because that's what we want our deodorant to do, turn our families on.

So, they pair me up with a girl at the audition and we do this thing. Afterward they were like, "You guys were great, please wait outside." So we went outside and she says, "That was awkward." I'm like, "Yeah completely." Then she says, "How old are you?" And, I was twenty-one. And she says, "Oh, because I'm fifteen." I was like, "Oh my God!" Long story short, I got the job. I remembered the girl's name was Shira and when they called I said, "Could you tell me if Shira got the part?" Because, if she did, I wasn't going to do it. But they said no, she didn't get it. So, fine. I get to set and it's a *different* fifteen-year-old girl—with her mother there.

As I said, I don't really do anything in the commercial. I'm like, pushing her off me, resisting, but, still, the idea is so fucked up. I remember it being tough times and being like, well, it's a job. I gotta do it. Get through it. I remember the last take, the piece of shit, egomaniac director goes up to the girl and whispers something in her ear. I'm like, "I don't like whatever he just said, this is gonna be awful." So the last take, it starts the same, she does what she's supposed to do and she smells me, throws me down, but what wasn't the same was that she suddenly rips off my shirt, buttons go flying, and she starts licking my chest. It was the most disturbing thing that I've ever had happen. Afterward, the director's like, "Thanks for being a great sport, Derek," and I'm like, "Fuck you." It was my own personal shirt too. Because it was so low-budget. I remember the agreement was for the commercial to be internet-only for three months or something. But then they wanted to get it on TV. They had to ask my permission to move it. I told them no. I said there's no money in the world they could pay me. They knew what they were doing was wrong. It was fucking disgusting.

Oh my God. There are four different things wrong with that story. It starts with the idea. I think it was around this time that we met. I remember because you smelled so good. *Badum-ching!* **I feel like I met you and then two seconds later you booked a series regular on a TV show. How did that happen?**
Well, my first job ever on a TV show was on *Spin City* . . .

Me too!
The guy who wrote my episode was a guy named Tom Hertz. He liked what I did on *Spin City* and cast me in a TV show he wrote called *Back to Kansas*, which later became *Married to the Kellys*. It unfortunately got cancelled after a year. I don't think the ratings were awful. I just don't know if it was the best show. And I'm not ripping on it . . . I loved doing the show, and everyone involved.

After it was over, I remember I was at Target and a guy came up and said, "Man, you were on my favorite show. Why'd they cancel that?" and I was like, "Well, I don't know. Family shows are kinda hard. I guess any show is hard to keep on the air." And he said, "What was it called again?" and I said, "*Married—*" and he goes, "*Married with Children*! That's right. What's up, Bud Bundy?" That was the best ego check for me.

When you got here, things were moving fast. I mean, you got here at twenty and by twenty-two you've got an agent, a manager, you are doing commercials, performing at Second City, you've been on a television series. And then, it's cancelled. How did you deal with all that?
I remember when it was cancelled, I kinda felt like I let people down. I felt like my family was so excited, friends were so excited. I would

hear from people the night it aired every week, and then all of a sudden nothing. It just stopped. And then I remember I would talk about it too much, how I didn't understand why it got cancelled. Plus getting paid a lot of money and then all of a sudden no money. And, yeah, I was twenty-two. It was confusing and I had to figure out what I was gonna do next.

I kept auditioning but I kept getting auditions like "Stoned-looking guy number 4" and "Drunk-sounding guy number 7." I wasn't booking stuff. And, I have to admit, I started getting a little bitter. But I didn't want that. I decided, I'm not going to get bitter. I used to work for my father who had a tire company. I worked in the warehouse with my brother, so when I would get depressed, I would call my brother and he would put the phone down for me so I could hear the shipping tape going over the boxes. That was my alternative. Stick it out here or go back to shipping boxes. That was good motivation.

What did you do?
I decided I was going to prove that I'm more than just how I look or how I sounded. And that's when I started writing short films with my friends at Second City. That's when I really started thinking, "I'm gonna be okay." *This* is what I love. I love acting but I think I'm better at creating ideas and directing.

Is that how *Drunk History* got started?
Yeah, one night me and one of my best friends from Second City, Jake Johnson from *New Girl*, we were having an unemployed actors' night of drinking, talking about cool things like music and Otis Redding. Jake started trying to convince me that Otis Redding knew he was going to die before he got on the plane that unfortunately crashed. I mean, Jake was just trying so hard to convince me, saying Otis looked at his wife and said, "You take care, baby, Otis has got to go," and his wife is like, "I will, Otis, you take care," but Otis says, "No, baby, Otis has *got* to *go*." And all I could picture was Otis

moving his lips, but also looking at me like, this never fucking happened. So I thought maybe it would be cool to tape Jake telling that story again, but also reenact it. But, then I thought, maybe it should be more hardcore history.

I asked my friend Mark Gagliardi for a moment in history that he thought would work, and he said the duel of Aaron Burr and Alexander Hamilton. I had been friends with Michael Cera for a long time and when I told him the idea, he said he would love to play Alexander Hamilton. So he did and Jake played Aaron Burr. That ended up being the first one. That was 2007. It was just going to be a short for this show I was doing at Upright Citizens Brigade. There was no pressure on it. It was fun to just complete something. But then Jack Black saw it and said he wanted to do one as Ben Franklin, so I was like, alright, maybe one more time. It wasn't until I put it on the internet that it became like a thing.

The one I saw was with Don Cheadle and Will Ferrell and Zooey Deschanel.
That was the fifth or sixth one. That one won the 2010 Best American Short and Jury Prize at Sundance.

That's amazing! I think it's interesting to note that your success with *Drunk History* was slow growing. You shot the first one in 2007. Sundance wasn't until 2010. After Sundance did you take it around to pitch it to different places to become a TV show?
Yeah, yeah. During this time, I was also working on another show that I had sold to HBO. I never expected that *Drunk History* would be the thing that hit. The best story about pitching it, was when we took it to the History Channel. They said, we love the idea but do they have to be drunk? Yeah, that was their note. The premise was their note. We took it around to a lot of different places. I remember Comedy Central, it felt like they really believed in what it was, and believed it

had an audience. They allowed us to make the show that we wanted to make. I think it helped that we had a visual reference.

I was always inspired by Billy Bob Thornton and how he made *Sling Blade*, how he made and financed that movie based off of a short. I always feel like, if I'm going to sell something, I want to show a short. That would be my advice to people who want to pitch. Make it yourself and show it. Because it's a visual creation. Show them. And, more than anything, you have to prove that you're the only person that can make the show. Make people trust that you believe in it so much that you are the best and only person who can do it.

A great example I have of doing it yourself is when I did a show called *Derek and Simon*. Bob Odenkirk directed and we created it together with Simon Helberg. We shot a presentation of it on our own, and sold it to HBO based off the presentation. It didn't get picked up but it went to Sundance and later we did it for the website Super Deluxe. One of the best experiences of my life. Bob Odenkirk is and will always be my hero and mentor.

What advice would you give to a person who just got here?
One thing I wish someone told me when I moved out here was . . . there is NO secret to this business. This is a business that nobody . . . ***nobody*** understands. Once you accept that, you can do anything. Just be you and you'll be fine.

So, off of that, I think the best advice would be, slow down. Everything is going to be fine, breathe. Seriously, we don't know if we're gonna be here tomorrow so just focus on what you can do today. Get involved with classes and stay close to people that have just arrived as well. You might feel this desire to be friends with people at a higher level, but I think the only way to learn is from the bottom. The more people that you're with at the bottom, the more you'll grow. I can humbly say that one of the best things out here for me has been the people I've met. Just stay close to the ones that you can tell are here to protect you, because most aren't. And that's not a negative thing to say, it's just true.

Also, you don't have to be an actor. There are other things to do in the entertainment business if it's not working out. It's not for everybody and that doesn't mean you're not good, it just means there's something else for you. Maybe this sounds anti-actor but it's not, because it's something I didn't really think about until I forced myself to start writing and making my own stuff. I felt like all I want to do is be an actor, to perform. But, I started to realize, instead of waiting for parts, I could create them. Make your own stuff. There's no excuse not to be making your own stuff if you feel you're not being seen as an actor. Prove you can do it.

Finally, don't compare yourself to anybody. It's the hardest thing to do, to not compare. But, really, the worst thing you can do is compare yourself to anyone. I loved Chris Farley and I wanted to be Chris Farley and it took me years to realize . . . I'm not Chris Farley and I'll just be me. I think to be a working actor is to understand it's not gonna be fun all the time, because nothing is always fun. But if it's the thing that you go to sleep thinking about and wake up thinking about, then that's your heart and no one can touch your heart. Be you and no one can ever touch you. If you're yourself, no one can stop you.

REED BIRNEY

Actor Reed Birney at rehearsals in Tad Danielewski's New York acting workshop

I met actor Reed Birney in New York City in 2013. My husband needed a fifty-year-old actor to play the lead role in a play reading for some off-Broadway theaters. Lee's agent recommended Reed. "He's a veteran of the stage, a great actor," he said. "Everyone in the New York theater scene knows Reed." Reed did us a huge favor by saying yes. He blew us away in the reading, and we all became friends. Over the years I've learned his story.

In 1978, at the age of twenty-two, Reed was starring on Broadway in the hit play *Gemini*. After that, he says, "nothing happened for thirty years." But then in 2008 he was cast in the disturbingly dark off-Broadway show *Blasted* and that, he says, is what "changed everything." Reed struggled for forty years before hitting his stride. In 2016 he won a Tony Award for his role in the Broadway play *The Humans*. If you are looking for a tale of determination and persistence, this is it.

Tell me a little about your training. I know you attended Boston University but left before graduating.
I dropped out after sophomore year. I was very, very ambitious and impatient. I loved freshman year and I hated sophomore year. Almost from the first day.

I also felt, in my youthful arrogance, that they weren't taking me seriously at the school. They treated me like I was a kid. Now I look back on it; I weighed about thirty-five pounds and looked about nine years old, and so why would they take me seriously? I wouldn't take me seriously either. So I moved down to New York.

Why New York and not Los Angeles?
Halfway through sophomore year a guy came up to me and said they were doing a musical version of *Look Homeward, Angel* on Broadway, and said I should audition to play Eugene. I thought, well I will. Frances Sternhagen was a family friend and I wrote to her and asked if she could get me an audition, and she did. I snuck out of school one Wednesday, took the train down from Boston, auditioned at the producer's apartment on Seventh Avenue and 53rd Street. I went and sang and maybe read a scene. It went fine. I thought I'd gotten it. But looking back on it, they weren't interested in me.

I moved to New York anyway to study at Circle in the Square—which is where they were going to do *Look Homeward, Angel*. I became a student there so I could be in the play. So began this obsession with

Thomas Wolfe and *Look Homeward, Angel*. I started writing letters to the composer saying, you know, I *am* Eugene. Just madness.

Wait, let me make sure I understand: You auditioned at the producer's house, didn't hear anything, but dropped out of school anyway and moved to New York so you could attend Circle in the Square and started reading up on everything to do with the show . . . just in case?
Just in case.

How did that work out?
I started at Circle in the Square in the fall of '74, and I think maybe the second day I was there they announced they were going to do *Where's Charley?* instead. The production of *Look Homeward, Angel* was postponed for a year. (*Laughs*) So, in my mind, that just gave me more time to prepare.

They tell you they aren't doing the play but you're thinking, the part of Eugene could possibly still be yours.
Right. It's up for grabs. It could still be mine. And I'm working really hard on it. But, I drop out of Circle in the Square in December of '74 because I got my Equity card doing this children's theater tour which I got through *Backstage*. I had sent in my picture, went in, and sang a couple of songs. Terrible children's theater. Swiss Family Robinson set in America; nothing Swiss. We toured in a sad station wagon from Maine to New Orleans to Florida. Seven of us piled in there with no iPads or Walkmen or anything. We had to listen to the AM radio. The oldest guy in the company was forty. He was a Vietnam vet with serious PTSD. It was a very unhappy group.

Was there anything about it that was fun?
No. I think there were some laughs along the way, but all of us would attest to it being the worst nine months of our lives.

But you completed your contract. Did you ever consider quitting?
Yes. All the time. But I stayed.

What did you do next?
When I got back from the children's tour, I wrote one last letter to the composer of *Look Homeward, Angel* and I said, "Look, I hear you're doing the show out on Long Island, I'm not crazy anymore. If you still haven't cast it yet, call me."

I love how you won't give up on this! What did he say?
He called me in and I got asked to do the "backers auditions," which was basically singing the score for money people. We must have done ten or fifteen shows for potential backers that summer. What I didn't know was that everyone doing the backers audition was going to be in the show—except me. They had somebody else in mind for the role of Eugene who didn't want to do the backers auditions. So I was just a fill-in.

In the meantime, I got into a great acting class, with Sigourney Weaver and Mercedes Ruehl. I was in class for about seven years with these gals and it was fantastic. It really saw me through some rough emotional times. We did a showcase in '76 and Sigourney was in it and two of her friends from Yale came to see it. Sigourney was about to start a play right after this at Playwrights Horizons, maybe the second play ever at Playwrights, and they asked me to play her little brother. I was happy to do it. It was called *Gemini*. It was supposed to be just six performances at Playwrights Horizons. At the very last performance, a producer from Long Island came. He had just lost a play at his theater and he needed something to go in right away. So he picked us up to move out to Long Island. Sigourney left because she had another job. This is all pre-*Alien*. We did *Gemini* for a month out in Huntington, Long Island, and at the last show in Huntington, Lanford Wilson and Marshall Mason came because they'd lost a play at Circle Rep. So they moved us back into New York where we were a huge hit, couldn't get a ticket. And from there we moved to Broadway, and I was with the show for two years.

That's amazing! What you thought was just a little six-performance thing turned into a Broadway run. Good thing you weren't in *Look Homeward, Angel*!
Yeah, while we were rehearsing *Gemini* at Playwrights Horizons for our six-show run, they were rehearsing *Look Homeward, Angel* for a dinner theater out on Long Island. They hadn't cast me. I was devastated. I thought, "I'm stuck doing this stupid play *Gemini*. They're all living the dream, doing the play I wanted to do." I remember coming into rehearsal one day wailing, crying, "I'm in this stupid showcase and they're rehearsing . . ." Then, *Gemini* opens on Broadway, it's a huge success. I go out to see *Look Homeward, Angel* and it's terrible. It takes them an additional year to open on Broadway. I go to the opening night party of *Look Homeward, Angel*. I was there when the bad reviews came in. You know, they come in with the papers, read the bad reviews, the party is over, it clears out, and I'm left hugging all my friends as they're sobbing. They thought it was going to be a hit. Anyway, big lesson there about how you never, ever know. You just never, ever know. I certainly didn't.

Being on Broadway in *Gemini*, a hit show, was essentially your first professional theater experience. That is a pretty huge success right out of the gate.
In many ways, it was a terrible thing to happen to me for several reasons. One, it was such a big hit, but I had the least flashy role in the play. It was a real collection of oddballs, and I was like the normal guy. Kind of like Barry Bostwick in *Rocky Horror*. So all the flashy characters won awards and were plucked out to do other shows and I couldn't get another job. So I got wildly depressed. I was twenty-two and on Broadway in a big, hit show and I was miserable. Now I think

the twenties are very hard anyway. They certainly were my hardest decade. There was probably stuff I needed to deal with anyway, but for someone as ambitious and driven as I was, to have to deal with that stuff was very good and miserable. I think that was the first time I thought about leaving acting.

But you didn't. Why not?
I had already dropped out of school. I didn't have a degree. I would have had to start as a freshman, that is if I knew what else I wanted to do. I thought maybe I could be an architect at one point, but that's a lot of math. Not for me. Every time I would call home, my mother would say, "Don't you want to go back to college and study French?" How is that better than being an actor? I'm really gonna clean up if I'm a French teacher?

That's funny . . . I minored in journalism. It was my parents' idea. They thought I could be a news anchor. To them it was the perfect blend of "real job" and being on TV. As if being on TV, in any form, was the goal.
They think our impulse to be an actor is to get attention. And getting attention as a newscaster is the same as doing a play. I remember being with my folks once during college and we were at the beach and we ran into some old friends of theirs and they invited us in for a drink. They asked me what I did for a living and when I told them I was an actor, I saw this whole world of emotions cross over this woman's face. She pulled my mother aside as we were leaving and she said, "How do you feel about that?"

I also had an agent say to me once—and I think the world thinks this—"In this business you're either a star or you're a bum." This was *my* agent. Well I'm not quite a star so I guess I'm a bum! How does it feel representing a bum? And I think the world thinks that.

So, what happened after *Gemini*?
Gemini ended and then I was just another schmuck actor kicking around. Gene Lasko was an Actors Studio guy, and he was Arthur Penn's producer and right-hand man, and Arthur was doing a movie written by Steve Tesich, who had just won the Oscar for *Breaking Away*. It was called *Four Friends* and it followed three guys and a girl through the '60s as they grew apart and came together. Gene brought me in to audition and I got it. It was a fantastic part. If the movie was a three-act play, my story was the second act. I was the lead guy's college roommate. And I had multiple sclerosis; it was a real Tiny Tim kind of role. But it was beautifully written and I got to do great stuff. But, I got that on my own. My agents had no real sense of what it was. I think they negotiated the deal but they hadn't submitted me for it.

Was this your first film? Was that part of your plan? To do both theater and film?
(*Laughs*) Oh yeah, I was going to be a big movie star.

It seems like you are headed in that direction, right? I mean, this is a hugely anticipated movie from an Academy Award–winning writer. It doesn't get better than that. Are you hitting the big time now?
So I do the film and I have an amazing time. It's going to come out in December of '81. In September of '81 I took a chance and went to Sam Cohn, who was the king of all agents at that point—he was Meryl Streep's agent and Sigourney's agent, he was Mike Nichols' agent and Woody Allen's agent. He was everybody's agent. He was Arthur Penn and Steve Tesich's agent so he was very involved with *Four Friends*, he's seen rough cuts and things—and I said, "I would like to work with you." And he said I had to get out of my contract with my other agent first. I immediately called up my agents and told them I was leaving and then signed with Sam.

Four Friends opens in December and every agent in America called me up after it opened and said they wanted to work with me. People were saying I was going to be nominated for an Oscar, blah blah blah. I said to all these people that I'd just signed with Sam Cohn and they said good luck, knowing they couldn't compete with that. And then, the movie tanked. It makes some people's ten-best list and some people's ten-worst list. Really crazy. Nobody was lukewarm on it. They either loved it or hated it. Mostly people hated it. Had the movie been a hit, Sam would have been the perfect place to be because he would help me field offers.

But because the movie tanked, I spent a year without a single audition. Not one. I didn't work for a year. And I would keep calling Sam to ask if I should be worried, and he'd say, "No, not yet. Not yet." But after a year of nothing, I felt like the ship had sailed. So I started calling a lot of those other agents back and they were like, no, the moment's gone. I'd been in a big Broadway play and had a lead in a major motion picture but none of it mattered. It was very hard. Because I really felt like I'd screwed up. I gambled with the Sam Cohn thing and I'd lost.

That sounds awful. Crushing. What did you do?
I was doing parts out of town and I got really depressed. I got really, really sad. I'm like, well I'm off to St. Louis to do *Merry Wives of Windsor*. Okay. And then you're gone for three months in the winter time and nobody cares that you were doing that thing. You might as well have taken a trip for all the good it did your career.

So in May of '85, I'm thirty-one years old, and I was walking up Broadway after a particularly gruesome audition, and a little voice said to me, "Go around the world. Take a trip." My grandmother had died in '84 and left me a chunk of money, so I took that money and I moved to Paris where I lived for five months. And then I took off with a backpack and traveled around the world. By myself. I had to do it to survive. I think of it now as a sabbatical but it really saved my life. The point of the trip was to see all the things I wanted to see but never let myself see because I was in this dysfunctional relationship with show business.

Did it seem like just a break or was there a chance you might not return to acting?
The point of the trip was to see things. The second point of the trip was to figure out what I was going to do. If I could figure out how not to be an actor, that would be great. And I kept a pretty rigorous journal. That was my travel companion. And there were rough days when it was very lonely and I remember just before I left, I was at a dinner party with friends and everybody knew I was going on my trip, and they were talking about auditions or some terrible show business thing and I was like, "So long, suckers!" and one of the guys turned to me and said, "Reed, you can run but you can't hide." And I remember waking up in paradise one day—I think it was Bali—and being really depressed. And I thought, oh, this has nothing to do with show business. This has nothing to do with my agents or a role or anything. This is me. This is my inability to find joy where I am. But also in Bali, I was in a corn field one day, writing in my journal, and I had this epiphany: that I am an actor. For better or for worse. This go 'round, I'm an actor. There's really nothing to be done. And that was a fantastic day, needless to say. I came back from the trip, I felt amazing, completely alive and invigorated.

Were things different when you got back?
Amazingly, one of the things I'd always wanted to do was grow my hair because I'd always had to be this clean-cut kid. So I grew it out on the trip. When I got back, my hair was down to my shoulders, and my first audition when I got back was at Playwrights Horizons and I showed up and was sitting on the little sad folding chairs with my hair down to here and a guy who was always at my auditions showed up and he said, "Hey, Reed, how you doing? What's going on?" And I thought, "I've been away for a year. I've been around the world. I can't

even begin to tell you what's going on." And I also realized if I hadn't gone around the world for a year, I'd still be sitting on this chair next to him. With short hair.

But, I got a wonderful job when I got back, *The Common Pursuit*, one of the greatest jobs I've ever had. I did that for six months and then back to back plays in Cincinnati and Louisville—just right back to the journeyman actor life.

So you aren't this huge success like you anticipated in your twenties, but you're working. At least you are working.

I was always working but they weren't particularly interesting parts. I'd have these great experiences or not-so-great experiences, but nothing ever changed. At that point, I'd been an actor for twenty-something years, and there were a fair amount of people who were like, "Hang in there, it's gonna happen," and I was like, there's no guarantee that it's gonna happen. I'm already kinda old. And I think if it was gonna happen, there probably would have been some indication. But there wasn't.

How did you deal with that? What advice would you give to an aspiring actor in the same situation?

The big shift for me was that I met Connie [Reed's wife] and I started to have a family, and that started to change things just in terms of my life. My career wasn't any better, but the rest of my life was. So what I would say to somebody is that it's so important to cultivate everything else. My problem was that I didn't have anything else. So that was a huge shift.

And then the big shift in my career was in 2006 I did a play at a major New York theater. I had seven lines. It was not a good play. It was not a play I was interested in. I did it because I'd auditioned for it and been cast and felt like I should work in this uptown theater because I had always worked off-Broadway. So I thought this would be good for me. It was a disaster. The lesson I learned there was, okay,

Reed, the dream didn't come true, so stop trying to go for it. Stop taking parts because you think it's a career move. You just gotta play parts that are interesting to you. At that point, I realized that I was kind of on the other side of the mountain.

How old were you when you had that realization?
I was fifty-two.

How did it change you?
I thought, I probably have twenty-five years left as an actor. If those twenty-five years go as quickly as the first twenty-five years I'm looking at a very specific set of coupons. So the new rule had to become "Is this a project I want to spend a coupon on?" And that made a huge difference psychologically for me. I wasn't trying to play the game. I really was choosing roles based on interest. Within the year came *Blasted*, which is the play that changed everything.

It primarily changed things for me artistically in that I was so scared of it—on page three I take off all my clothes and say to the girl, "Put your mouth on me." That's page three! And I just thought, how can I do this thing? It literally made me sick to my stomach, that's how scary it was to me. And I thought, well you have to do it if it scares you that much. You need to do that play.

And when I took my clothes off, like the fourth day of rehearsal, and I didn't die, I thought, "I can do this." It was incredibly empowering. It wasn't a part I would have gone to see and thought, "Why wasn't I seen for that?!" I felt like Superman after that. And that is what changed mostly; there was a confidence and fearlessness since *Blasted*. And it didn't hurt that everybody in the world saw it. It ran three months and it really changed everything.

Reed was nominated for a Drama Desk Award for his performance in *Blasted* and has gone on to receive a Tony nomination for his work in *Casa Valentina* (2014), and in 2016 won the Tony Award for his role in *The Humans*. He has also appeared in the critically acclaimed off-Broadway production of *Uncle Vanya*, the Broadway production of *Picnic*, and has a recurring role on Netflix's *House of Cards*. In 2016 he was honored with a caricature at Sardi's—which is basically a theater actor's version of a star on the Hollywood Walk of Fame. It only took him forty years.

During his acceptance speech at the Tony Awards, he said, "I've been an actor for almost forty-two years, which I cannot believe I am saying. Thirty-five of them were pretty bad and, that's a lot of them. I just couldn't get anything going. The last eight have been great, but the thing that was always great wherever I was, whatever level I was on, were the amazing people I got to work with. Almost all of them were hilarious and talented and full of passion and joy and they loved putting on plays and telling stories. They always have been and are still the best part of what I do and I am so grateful to all of you and I love sharing the planet with all of you. Thank you very much."

ADVICE FROM PEERS

I was recently asked to speak at an actor's workshop in Los Angeles. I told them I was writing this book and asked what they wish they knew when they began their journey and what advice they could pass on to those just getting started. Here is what they said:

"Give yourself time to figure out who you are."

"Get mentally prepared. If you come with a deadline, that can trip you up. Mentally play the long game. Don't get hung up on timelines. I had a great agent and was getting great auditions, but I wasn't ready. Now I wish I'd known I wasn't ready."

"I wish I'd taken more advantage of the years before I moved out here and worked on my reel and résumé. I'm doing those things now. I'm from South Carolina and I wish I'd auditioned there and taken advantage of that market."

"Being in class makes you a working actor, even though you're not getting paid."

"Auditioning *is* the job—best advice I've gotten."

"An audition doesn't mean everything else in my life stops. I still have to go to class or to work and the audition is just another part of my day."

Advice from Peers

"You get paid a lot of money on the days you work to make up for the days that you don't. Save it."

"Ninety percent of the readiness is believing in yourself."

"You're the commodity. Treat yourself well."

"Make your own work and write a role you want to play if you're not getting cast."

"Check your ego, and be open to learning."

PHOTO CREDITS

Page 35: Photo by E. Charbonneau/WireImage/Getty Images
Page 40: Photo by Ron Rybkowski
Pages 41, 43, 44, 45: Photos by Tama Rothschild Deitch
Page 46: Photo by Paul Gregory
Page 47: Photo © Susan Maljan
Page 109: Photo by Paul Smith/Featureflash
Page 126, 153, 158: Photos by Derek Waters
Page 132: Photo by Allison Jones
Page 137: Photo by NBC/NBCUniversal/Getty Images
Page 143: *Walk Hard: The Dewy Cox Story* © 2007 Columbia Pictures Industries, Inc. and GH Three LLC. All Rights Reserved. Courtesy of Columbia Pictures.
Page 152: Photo by Kim Ferry
Pages 156, 159, 166: Photos by Angela Kinsey
Page 173: Photo by Nick Holmes
Page 201: Photo by Chanel Cook
Page 206: Photo by Isabel Richardson
Page 238: Photo by Algis Kaupas
Personal photos provided by Jenna Fischer.

ACKNOWLEDGMENTS

As with most creative projects, this book exists thanks to the efforts of many people. This is where I get to thank them.

Thank you to my parents, Jim and Anne Fischer, my first cheerleaders; and the first to believe that I really could do this crazy acting thing.

Thank you Richard Abate and Naomi Odenkirk for trusting in this project and helping me to make it a reality. It was seven years between our first phone call and a finished manuscript.

Thank you Glenn, Monica, Debbie, Leah, Sarah, Adrienne, Jennifer, and everyone at BenBella for your guidance, support, and enthusiasm.

Thank you to my artistic circle of readers and advice givers: Michelle Gunn, Trevor Algatt, Lindsey Schuberth, Gia Crovatin, and Robert D'Avanzo.

Thank you Aynsley Bubbico for transcribing all of my lectures and interviews.

Thank you Naomi Odenkirk (again), Allison Jones, and Mara Casey for your insider information. (A special thanks to Allison for going to her storage unit to find the original casting Breakdown for Pam Beesly.)

Acknowledgments

Thank you Reed Birney, Sean Gunn, Derek Waters, and Natalie Zea for letting me share your stories.

Thank you Weston and Harper Kirk for visiting me in my office 12 times a day as I wrote this book. I loved every time you knocked on the door.

And most of all, thank you to my husband Lee Kirk, a professional writer, who read every draft, edited every story, and polished every joke in this book for me. He took my clumsy writing and turned it into something readable. You've earned a free pass for the next five Valentine's Days.

(Note: If this page seems clunky it's because I didn't let Lee edit it. I wanted it to be a surprise.)

ABOUT THE AUTHOR

Jenna Fischer is best known for playing Pam Beesly on the acclaimed television show *The Office*, for which she received an Emmy nomination for Best Supporting Actress and two SAG Awards for Outstanding Performance by an Ensemble Comedy.

After wrapping *The Office*, Fischer went on to star in the UK/SKY B limited series *You, Me and the Apocalypse* along with Rob Lowe and Megan Mullally. She also starred in the off-Broadway play *Reasons to Be Happy*, written and directed by Neil LaBute. Most recently, Fischer was onstage in the world premiere of Steve Martin's newest absurdist play *Meteor Shower* for a record-breaking run at the Old Globe Theatre.

Fischer's film credits include *The Giant Mechanical Man* (which she also produced), The Farrelly brothers' comedy *Hall Pass*, *Solitary Man*, opposite Michael Douglas, *Walk Hard: The Dewey Cox Story*, produced by Judd Apatow, and *Blades of Glory*, opposite Will Ferrell. She is upcoming in the Mike White feature *Brad's Status* starring Ben Stiller and *The 15:17 to Paris* directed by Clint Eastwood.